40 Years Wandering

How God Directed My Steps
Into a Life of Surrender

Sabrina Faubel

For Jules, Mom, and Traci.
The three of you are the only ones who understand what was lost when we lost Dad. You have supported every piece of this work and every piece of me. I could never thank you enough, and I could never love you more.

Table of Contents

Foreword

If you needed an honest, unbiased perspective on a situation, who would you turn to? That one friend who loves you enough to tell you how it is? Or perhaps that family member who is unashamed to be themselves and call it like they see it? Possibly someone who communicates in sarcasm mixed with grace? For us, it's Sabrina.

Our church places a large importance on small groups coming from the belief that "church happens in circles in living rooms, not in rows in a building". We've had the privilege of leading one of those groups weekly, and Sabrina has been a part of that group since 2019. She has brought a wealth of Bible knowledge, personal experience, authenticity, wit, vulnerability and, yes, sarcasm week in and week out. She's helped create an environment where people are comfortable coming as they are to offer reflections or simply listen and learn from one another. But Sabrina's greatest contribution to our group (and our own lives) has not been her words. She is a doer. She doesn't just reflect and move on. She moves to action. As she does, she teaches, challenges, and encourages those around her to do the same.

Our home is at the end of a cul-de-sac with very little parking space. So, when we have 15 people over to our home every week, parking gets a little hectic, and the cul-de-sac fills right up. During a study about neighborly love, we started reflecting on our own shortcomings reaching out to our neighbors. We confessed this to our group and asked them to walk alongside us as we sought to improve. Sabrina took it upon herself to keep us accountable by making thank you bags which included sweets and letters to each of our neighbors explaining how grateful we are for their willingness to let us commandeer the street weekly. The letters went on to explain why we gather in fellowship as a response to the love of God. She brought them to our home the next week and our job was simply to hand them out.

As a middle school teacher in a (challenging) public school system, Sabrina also has the opportunity to be a voice in the lives of hundreds of students each year. And if you've ever been around a bunch of 12 and 13 year olds, you know the value (read: necessity) of being direct. Sabrina has become a master at it. Her willingness to bring the same unashamed bluntness she needs in the classroom into this book makes it not only a quick read, but a tangible and practical one as well.

As we read through the book, it was remarkable how much it felt like having a conversation with our friend. She pours her personality onto the pages with the same sarcasm, wit, and authenticity that we've come to know, expect, and cherish from our sister. And as expected, she doesn't pull any punches. The conversational tone she writes with makes the book approachable and relatable to readers regardless of their own background or life experiences. With that said, both of us immediately remarked at how much of our own lives, stories, and inner monologues had parallels to hers. At times, it was as if she had looked into our own hearts and took the words from our lips.

Because of its approachability and voice, the book successfully uncovers and explains important spiritual truths (the Lordship of Christ, and the relationship between justification and sanctification to name a couple) without getting bogged down in theological or academic terminology. It's filled with personal experiences, Bible excerpts, insightful reflections, and practical challenges. The style of writing makes it just as accessible in a diner in the Bible Belt as it is in an office in Silicon Valley.

While we think that anyone could find value and enjoyment in reading this book (and we pray that all who read these words will), it is particularly valuable for anyone who grew up in a "Christian" home, community, culture, or context. Those of us who come from such backgrounds are in danger of becoming desensitized, jaded, or even numb to the beauty of the Gospel, the sovereignty of God, the magnitude of the call to surrender, and the command to personal holiness. As you read Sabrina's journey towards surrender in the book, you will find yourself examining your own life and will be invited to share with her in doing the same.

As our friend says in her introduction, the book is not written that you would agree with her in every way. It is written that you might see God's love on display in her life and that you might see and believe that He extends that same love to you. We pray that as you read through the book you will be drawn to the magnificence of the love of Christ, and you will offer your surrender to His will knowing that His love never fails.

Sincerely,
Aaron & Mariah Moger

Introduction

The need to travel my own path is rooted in me. It is so deeply rooted that, at times, I've knowingly chosen a more difficult route just to be able to say it was my own and not the same as others. While the world may say, "You do you, boo," the reality is that this desire stems from sin in my heart that calls to me like a siren, telling me that my way is greater than God's way. It is pride, and the journey I choose will always be in vain.

For many years I traveled from place to place with a fear that I would eventually settle down (*yikes*) and become one of those uninteresting people who followed the American dream straight into a soccer-mom SUV, living in a cul-de-sac (double *yikes*). The desire to rebel against the status quo has never fully left my spirit, and there are times when I still feel ill at ease paying a mortgage and buying groceries from the same store every week. But despite my shortcomings, God has seen fit to meet me where I am, guide my wandering spirit through the wilderness, and set me firmly in the promised land.

If you're unfamiliar with this idea of a promised land (or if you've forgotten the story) it goes something like this: The Israelites, God's chosen people, were freed from slavery in Egypt under the leadership of Moses, whom God had sent as a spokesperson. There is a gripping story of Moses, Pharaoh, and the Red Sea in the book of Exodus. It is a must-read. Suffice it to say that the Israelites were freed and began a journey to the promised land. This land that God had promised to them is often called the "land flowing with milk and honey." (Ex. 3:8, 17; 13:5; 33:3) It would be the best the earth had to offer and, while there would be some challenges before they could fully inhabit the land, they would always be under God's protection and provision. Can we say, "Jackpot"?

Alas, things got a little sticky not long after the fantastic rescue. The Israelites fell into a pattern of turning to God and then away from God. They allowed God to have control and then found they liked living outside of his rules much better. Ultimately, God disciplined them by making a promise that none of the original Israelites over the age of twenty would be allowed into the promised land. This is, of course, due to a list of sins that they allowed to come between themselves and God. Because God is faithful and just, the Israelites wandered in the wilderness for forty years until God brought them to the long-awaited promised land.

Over the past year, I've been experiencing my version of the promised land. I am now in my forty-first year of life, and so it is easy to draw parallels between my choices and those of the Israelites from long ago. The following chapters are my account of my own wandering in the wilderness, which, incidentally, lasted about forty years. Now that I am a year into understanding what it looks and feels like to actually surrender to the will of God, I desire to share my story in the hopes that it will resonate with someone else. We are not alone in the wilderness. Our journeys may look and sound different, but we are all sinners in need of the redeeming love of Christ.

Before you begin reading about the mishaps and mistakes that brought me to my current season in life, it could be helpful if you have an idea of where this is going. My story probably looks similar to that of any other believer who has surrendered their life to the will of God. If you're not a believer in Christ, then some of the words and phrases I use might seem odd to you. That's okay. Honestly, from the outside of any circle, the inside can be hard to understand. What my heart wants you to hear is that God loves us—me *and* you. There is a God who actually desires to love you, guide you, and spend time with you. This is not a wishing-well god who I just seek out when I have a list of requests to make my life more comfortable. This is *the* God. The only one who chases after us instead of *us* trying to chase after *him*.

And if this sounds a little backward or awkward, it's okay. Read on. Take what you can use from my story. I don't mind. A common mistake in our current culture is that we have to immediately dismiss an entire person or idea if we disagree with even a part of them. I submit this to you: finish the book. Glean from it what you can use in your own life and let the rest fall away.

Now, go grab a snack. We have some wandering to do.

Chapter 1

Acting the Part

At the age of eight, I was sitting in Sunday school listening to my teacher, Mrs. Montgomery, explain the details of how to become a Christian. When we bowed our heads to pray, I followed along with her and asked God to forgive me for my sins and save me. The prayer ended, and I felt good. I then promptly kept the whole thing to myself. I think it was because it just felt a bit cliché. (Though I didn't know that word, I definitely knew the intention behind it.) It just felt like the same thing everyone else did. It seemed redundant to share about it happening again. Same story - different kid.

It was the late 80s and I attended a United Methodist church in the heart of Illinois. Looking back, I realize not only the significance of that prayer of salvation, but also how many pieces God must have put in place for me to be led there. My parents both attended church regularly, and we (my three siblings and I) were taught to do the same. I do not remember hearing about salvation, though, any other time in my childhood until we moved to the South and began visiting a Southern Baptist church. The stark contrast between these two houses of worship

is not lost on me. In one, we rarely spoke of salvation or tes-
timonies. In the other, we threw those terms around so much
I'm fairly certain I became desensitized to the whole thing after
a while. Words are incredibly important, as are when and how
often they are used.

What I now know is the importance of that moment in Mrs.
Montgomery's class. It was my first step out of the invisible chains
that sin had created in my life. Which, admittedly, sounds really

> **Over the last thirty-two years, I've watched many people accept Christ and then feel the burden of acting like a Christian.**

deep for an eight-year-old. That's
why it is something I see now and
not something I really understood
back then. Back then, it just meant
that I had to officially start acting
like a Christian—publicly. To be
honest, it's probably the point when
I no longer acted like a Christian—
in my heart. I say that mostly because it was just before I began my
preteen years, a time in my life when
God, in his infinite wisdom and
mercy, was going to allow me to be

exactly who I wanted with the ultimate plan of drawing me closer
to himself many years later.

Over the last thirty-two years, I've watched many people accept
Christ and then feel the burden of acting like a Christian. May
I share something I've learned? In any area of your life, if you
have to act like something or someone, it's not genuine, and the
rest of us will only be fooled for so long. No one can keep up an
act forever. It's the equivalent to carrying a secret that everyone
wants to know. You'll dance around the issue, pretend it doesn't
exist, and even avoid talking about it. It will be this fantastic
practice in lying. At the end, all it does is make you better at

lying. It's better to just go ahead and dispense with the acting now. Go ahead. I'll wait.

If you're confused, let me help clarify. "Acting the part" means we go to church, read the Bible, tell people we'll pray for them, sound off a *hallelujah* when something good happens, and give credit to "the man upstairs." It can also look like leading worship, teaching Sunday School, or driving the church van every Sunday and Wednesday. Further still, it can be saying that we are blessed, being a great employee, and being known for helping everyone with anything. What we need to remember is that none of these things will bring us closer to God if we have not already given him our hearts. It's all a ruse to impress others and even ourselves. If you think about it, I could conceivably do none of the things listed above . . . and still call Jesus my Lord and Savior. It's all acting. Of course, I didn't fully realize this my whole life. I have no idea who around me might be acting a part like this. In fact, I think that we are often in this trap of playing a part and we don't even see it in ourselves. I had heard it. I believed it. And I even told others about it. But true surrender didn't come until after my fortieth birthday.

To be abundantly clear—asking Jesus to forgive your sins and attempting to walk in his ways is a genuine offering on our part. When we make this commitment, we are saved and will one day be with him in heaven. I don't want anyone to misunderstand the title of this chapter and think that salvation is something to balk at, or worse, that salvation is something you can only achieve after a magical experience of walking on water. Admitting you are a sinner, acknowledging that Jesus died on the cross to pay for those sins, and asking the Holy Spirit to lead you starting today are the steps to salvation and eternal life in heaven—no question about it.

The journey I'm describing in this chapter and the ones that follow is my experience *after* being saved. It is me trying to openly say that I really did think I was following Jesus all of my days and I had questions about why the pieces didn't seem to fit and why I had such a hard time following him. It was my stubbornness and pride that led to my not reaching my full potential as a child of God. He was waiting for me, ever so patiently, leaving a breadcrumb trail that I refused to follow. I'm hoping that maybe my story will resonate with someone who is where I once was. I'm hoping that somehow, in God's infinite mercy, someone will read these words and find the path to surrender in their own life. Salvation was the best single event to happen to me, but surrender is the best way I can think of to live out the rest of my days.

May I share another secret with you? I spent a lot of years thinking I had surrendered. I wondered why something still felt a little fake. I wanted to know if this is all there was to the Christian life. I asked if I'd ever really love reading the Bible. I wondered so many things and it didn't make sense to me because I had prayed and read

I spent a lot of years thinking I had surrendered.

and studied. What was I not getting? Why didn't my faith have an enduring presence? I now know it's because I was acting. I had experienced such great examples of faith in my life that I learned to emulate them very well. I had fooled everyone.

Almost everyone. I think my dad knew. And I think deep down I knew, too. During those years of salvation without surrender my playwriting skills became so well-honed that I almost forgot all of my questions about what seemed off. There was one glaring issue in my life that I was able to avoid for so long: I did not know how to close the curtain on the play and start living the real thing.

My play was incredibly well-scripted (if I do say so myself). Y'all. Seriously. I'm a writer, and I have written more stories in my head than I can count. My biggest masterpiece was the tale I had woven using the imaginary thread that I told myself was accurate. I don't write plays, as a general rule, but the drama I created in my life would have been titled, *Pride and Prejudice: The True Story of How I Judged Others, Misjudged Myself, and Couldn't Have Been Prouder of It.*

Our leading lady would be me as an eight-year-old. A girl who wanted to please her parents so badly that she adopted their faith as her own. Though her salvation was authentic, her faith was underdeveloped. As she grew into a teenager, she was bitter toward everyone. She wanted to live in isolation but was taught to love others, so she tried. She worked hard to help everyone (which she enjoyed), get good grades (which she was proud of), and present herself to the world as a well-put-together young lady (which she was—fifty percent of the time). All of this she did because it was just how her family believed people should behave. And all of the family beliefs were rooted in biblical teaching. There is no way that someone outside of the family would ever question the true intentions of this fine, upstanding young person.

On the inside, though, our heroine was sarcastic and spiteful. She took all of the negative energy she was hiding from the world and focused it on her family behind closed doors. She threw tantrums when she was unhappy with a decision, spent hours making fun of her sister—whom she viewed as inferior in intelligence—and rebelled against her parents. As she grew into a teenager, her friends were confused by how easily she could attach and detach herself from people. There was a facade of vulnerability, but she kept her true self tucked away so that no one could really hurt her.

Unfortunately, all of these characteristics just continued to grow stronger as she grew older. God placed terrific people around her who loved her in spite of all of this. They loved our leading lady even when she would talk to them every day for a week and then not reach out again for six months. They loved her even though her sarcasm could be incredibly hurtful and unnecessary. They loved her even though she often put her job ahead of all other things because she believed teaching was a greater calling than all else. She was self-centered, arrogant, and believed that it was all balanced out because, at the end of the day, she helped people and was a decent person.

What does your play look like?

Let me give some examples if you're still unsure whether or not you're acting.

In My Teen Years:

"You have such a lovely daughter. She is so responsible," gushed the woman who I had just helped up the steps at church. This was not uncommon for my parents to hear when it came to their children. My parents were both raised in loving, disciplined homes and they believed in raising us the same. We had a good structure, firm boundaries, and an abundance of love and support. I learned early on that if someone truly cares for me, they will call out my mistakes and also compliment my strengths.

Because I heard the line about being responsible so often, I had a strong desire to show that characteristic as often as possible. Who wouldn't? I was acting responsibly for the satisfaction of people noticing my being responsible. This is different from acting responsibly because it is the right thing to do (which is a better reason, but still not the best reason). How about I act responsibly because God calls me to handle my business and be a good steward of the gifts I've been given? How about I act responsibly not under obligation but as an outpouring of my love for Christ and the power of the Holy Spirit on days when it is uncomfortable to do so? Heart posture and motivation are a pretty big deal. I didn't understand that, yet.

Inside, during my pre-surrender days, I was judging anyone who did not show responsibility to the same degree as I did. I kept a running tally of people in my life who failed to meet my expectations. I wasn't always aware of this, of course; it's only been since my divine intervention experience that I realize how awfully judgmental I've been my entire life. What's even more ridiculous is how people I

> **Heart posture and motivation are a pretty big deal.**

love have pointed this out to me and I agree with them but then say, "I'm working on it," as if I have any control over it. That's the difference between wandering and promised-land living; the former is a constant struggle to do what's right. The latter is filled with the beauty of knowing that I can never do what's right—in my own power. It will always require the power of the Holy Spirit inside of me.

In my Career:

"She's my favorite teacher," a student relays to his mom at the grocery store after bumping into me. The mom smiles and goes on about how I'm the only teacher she knows about because he's always talking about how much he likes my class. I smile politely and utter something to make me sound humble. That something can sound like "Oh, goodness. I'm sure there are others"; "You don't have to say that. I'm sure you secretly have a different favorite," or even, "You're too kind. I just try to do my job." None of these are inherently evil. But the intention behind it and the place from which these words flowed weren't quite right. My pride slowly became over-inflated while my confidence in my skills wavered constantly. I worked hard to maintain the things I was good at and avoided things I found difficult. That meant countless hours reading about, preparing for, and buying things for teaching. I spent time I didn't have and money that didn't belong to me (debt is a terrible master) to further a career that I was making into an idol. Life sneaks up on us in that way. Careers, family members, community, and many more things that are simply blessings can quickly become idols. We don't see it.

Meanwhile, it was always the same story when I'd attend Sunday school or a Bible study—"I'm struggling with pride (or doubt or fear or consistency)." Either that or I'd just spout off all of the facts I knew from whatever chapter we were reading. I was never really *struggling* with those issues. I was just acknowledging they existed. I would occasionally get upset that I was burdened with them. The only reason I ever struggled was because I was trying so hard to act out what I wanted to be. I inevitably walked away from Bible studies and other things frustrated because no one had any new insight and here I was spending time teaching everyone else what I knew. I'll admit this was not always the case, but it seemed to be a pattern with most studies I attended. I see now how this was not a problem with the leaders or other members. It was a problem with my heart posture. I don't know if I didn't want to be challenged or if I just felt like I really had all of the basics down.

Something else I've learned—through surrender and two years of counseling—is that I don't like being vulnerable. I'm assuming most people are not super comfortable with being vulnerable. But if we mix an above-average level of pride (which runs rampant in my life) and a disdain for vulnerability, we get someone who learns how to share just enough and make others feel safe but never truly feels safe herself. It was this combination that led to my putting so much trust in my parents that I didn't even try to trust anyone else. This became a difficult thing to admit when I realized the damage it has done in many relationships—including, but not limited to my failed marriage. God has used counseling to reveal some deep patterns in my life. He has also used it to show me that in order to become more like him, we must first let him chisel out the parts of us that keep us in our sin, then take time to let him heal those wounds.

Aside from counseling, though, I think it's probably evident at this point how God used my parents as a source of accountability. There were so many ways in which my parents did a great job of raising four children. The thing I remember most is the consistency and commitment with which they attended church and spent time in the Word.

"Are you reading your Bible?" If you ask any of my siblings they'll agree that this was a common question from Dad. It was his way of nudging us without pushing too hard. Whenever we'd be stressed or wondering what to do about a situation, he'd open with that question. It's a great question.

"Are you reading your Bible?"

And one that I lied about when answering more often than not. I was reading my Bible—at church when it was absolutely required. I was reading my Bible—at Bible study when it was absolutely needed. I was reading my Bible—in front of the Christmas tree each year as we shared the story from Luke 2. Reading my Bible wasn't going to save me—I was already saved. Why did I need to reread stories I'd already read? I heard it brought people closer to God, but I'd much rather read a novel, and I'd much rather paint my room, and I'd much rather just not have to be bored into sleep.

There were moments when I truly desired to start reading my Bible more. I bought countless devotional books, each time thinking I was going to really start reading. I set up calendars and made plans, only to end up sleeping in or "needing" to do something else. And every single time I rationalized, "Reading my Bible is not what saves me. I'm already saved. It's just a perk that I'm opting out of."

I'm sharing because I know there are others out there in the same space. You can judge me and pretend to be shocked, but I know the truth. You got that cup of coffee started, did some stretching while you waited for it to brew, and then carried on with your day—only to realize fifteen minutes later that you had not done your morning devotional. You tell yourself you'll do it later. And then later comes, and you still don't make time. And then you say you'll do it before bed, but sleep is too needed. Of course, you maybe could have squeezed it in while you watched the latest episode of that show you've been streaming. But that would have taken away from time with your spouse. You could have done it while you were fixing dinner, but what if the kids may have possibly needed you? You could have done it on your lunch break at work. But that would invite questions from co-workers or require you to not listen to the podcast that helps you relieve stress from work. I'm not stupid. And neither are you. We can always come up with reasons to run from things that are uncomfortable or that we don't really want to do. Even children figure out from the age of two how to avoid vegetables. Let's stop being toddlers.

In fact, let's go ahead and throw out another sore spot: prayer time. If I'm going to lose readers, I might as well get rid of them in the first chapter.

What did my prayer life look like before surrender? Well, it was definitely basic and involved a lot of genie-esque requests. It usually started with: "Heavenly Father, please be with _____ during her surgery. Grant traveling mercies (if you're not from the South, you may not understand this one) to _____ as she visits Disney World this week. Help me study for this test that I kinda waited until the last minute to think about. Please relieve my stress. Thank you. Amen." This was my standard, once-a-week type prayer. It was usually on Sunday mornings when either Sunday school or the service required silent prayer time. I would bet that other people who have not yet learned about surrender have a similar prayer life. It's more like a prayer pedestal. We go up there once a week to make our requests and then come back down and live the rest of our lives separated from the place where wishes are granted. It's a bit sad.

We also prayed at meals. And sometimes before bed. When I had a child, I prayed before bed and before meals with her. I also followed some of the prayer habits I learned from my parents. There's something about becoming a parent that pushes you into a new realm of trying to be a better person. I think it's the sudden realization that this tiny human is now looking up to you for all of his/her social and emotional cues. At any rate, we prayed for ambulances or fire trucks that passed by. We prayed for wisdom and for Grandpa's healing. We prayed for the bugs outside or at nighttime when we were scared. Slowly I noticed that the only time I prayed was when I was with my child. So I didn't have my own prayer life. I had just graduated to recognize that I wanted my child to have a healthy prayer life. Not a big difference.

It wasn't precisely after the surrender that I began praying more and more passionately. It was in the midst of the transition that I went through that I felt closer to God when I sat still and prayed. When I became comfortable approaching him as God, I was also approaching someone who knew me so intimately that I could be myself. My prayers became about how I could be filled with more of the Holy Spirit and less of myself; how I could reach others with his love and not hoard it; what I needed to change or adjust in my life to be better aligned with his will for me. I still make requests, and I still bring my problems, but it is because I want to share things with the One who can help me sort them out, not fix them for me.

The *struggle* of reading my Bible and praying disappeared when those things became about digging into my relationship with my Savior. The Holy Spirit began to get bigger, and my desire to be anywhere else got smaller. There are days when I can physically feel myself being pulled toward God. It sounds absolutely ludicrous, but it happens. I don't even know how to describe it. My soul truly thirsts for more of it. I actually almost fear the day when I allow life to creep in and forget how wonderful it is to wake up in the morning and spend time with the One who made me.

So—Are you reading your Bible? Are you praying daily? Your answer is, of course, between you and God. He already knows the truth so you might as well confess it. You'll feel better. We must admit our shortcomings before we can begin a plan of action to address them. Start here. Start now.

> **Author Suggestion: Before you read any more of this book, get your Bible app (or— gasp!—the actual, physical Bible) and hold it in your lap. Bow your head and confess your sins. Ask for forgiveness. Ask God if he would be gracious enough to reveal himself to you while you read. Then choose a random chapter and read it. After you read, pray that the scripture will be brought to mind throughout your day so you can see how it applies to your life.*

Chapter 2

I'm Trying

"Clean your room," my mom would say in a loud huff of frustration.

"I'm trying," I would respond, in a whiny voice, while I continued to slowly pick up and play with each toy or examine each piece of paper before placing it aside.

Fast forward thirty years.

"I don't know why it's difficult to just clean your room," I say in a frustrated voice to my daughter.

"I'm trying," she responds in an equally frustrated voice (with an added eye roll for dramatic effect.) Then she picks up another piece of paper to closely examine it before setting it aside.

Children and adults often view tasks very differently. The one place where this is most consistently evidenced is in the process of cleaning a room. A child looks at a mess and feels overwhelmed, unsure of where to start or how to organize the cleaning process. Meanwhile, an experienced adult can immediately size up the situation and get the job done. Somewhere between childhood and adulthood, we forget what it felt like to be that overwhelmed child who so badly wants to please her parents but doesn't have the experience to accomplish the goal.

Throughout my life, I felt like I was having this conversation with God repeatedly. God would tell me to go and do. I would either resist or not hear because I was busy doing what I wanted. I consulted no one but myself for major life decisions (choosing a college, figuring out how to travel, etc.) and those decisions would eventually pile up and make a big, overwhelming mess. My life would become cluttered with all of my wants, and I'd feel out of control and not know how to get started cleaning it up. Thankfully, God is the perfect parent, and He comes along beside me and helps me sort through the messes I've made. Once surrender became a part of my life, I started to see how I can prevent the messes to begin with.

Remember when I mentioned that traveling is rooted in me? At the age of sixteen I decided to go on a mission trip to Brazil. (Notice how I said, "I decided," and not "God sent me"?) I read about this trip for teenage girls in a Christian magazine my grandmother had purchased for me. My life could not have felt more boring and when I saw that they were hosting a mission trip out of the country it took about two seconds to know what I wanted. As with most things in my younger years, the only thing I needed to do was decide I wanted it, and I'd find a way to make it happen. I approached my parents who looked incredibly hesitant but promised they would think about it and discuss it. Some time later Mom said she was fine with it, and Dad said he didn't think it was a good idea. To this day I don't know if that was an attempt at a good cop/bad cop routine and, to be honest, it didn't really matter. In the end, I got what I wanted after a long list of arguments I had prepared before we even started the second round of negotiations.

Even though I kind of always knew that it wasn't God calling me to go but more my will demanding that I leave my hometown, the Holy Spirit was working in me. There were moments on that trip when I felt God's presence and had glimpses of what it would be like to live a Holy Spirit-filled existence—when I was willing to let it happen. That's another thing about wandering enroute to the promised land. It incessantly feels like everything will come together at some point. And I have control over the coming together, but at the same time I can't figure out how to make it happen. In the lifetime leading up to surrender I can point to so many moments when I imagined that I had figured it out. I was sure I was letting God lead and I had given him everything. Upon reflection I think I can safely say that an indication of not fully surrendering was the fact that I felt wishy-washy at best. I'm definitely not perfect now, nor will I ever be. However, living in a more complete state of surrender puts me in a position in which the majority of my time is spent either being led by the Holy Spirit or quickly recognizing I'm not letting the Holy Spirit lead and re-surrendering. At the time of the Brazil mission trip, I may have considered asking for God to lead a couple of times a month, at most.

Returning from Brazil was a big letdown. I wanted to stay out of the country and in unfamiliar territory as long as possible. Reverse culture shock is incredibly real. It was difficult to sleep in a comfortable bed or have access to food 24/7 because I had experienced a life that did not include those luxuries. If I had not already been sold on traveling, that trip definitely solidified everything for me. Whatever happened in life, I would make a way to travel and see the world. Of course, I'd let God lead a few things and then ask for his blessing on the things I had already determined for myself. I was a good, Christian girl, after all.

I'm always wondering if it is God's will for me to stay in a particular season for a long while or a short while. Terms such as *longsuffering* raise the question, "How long is long?" Unlike most single women my age, I don't fully desire to be married, and I don't fully wish to be single. Prior to getting married I never really thought I wanted to get married or have children. I was incredibly blessed with the opportunity to have both. Considering that the life of surrender calls me to live day by day not knowing what comes next, I won't have answers to my questions until something happens. In the meantime, I'm doing my best to become the woman God wants me to be. That doesn't mean that I'm not distracted by pursuing my own interests from time to time. It does mean, however, that I have a much easier time recognizing distractions. And when things do not go how I may have thought I wanted, I have a much easier time letting go of what might have been. At the end of the day, my heart's desire is to follow my Savior, and he will lead me where I need to go. He will create relationship opportunities with those he has chosen, and he will protect me from those he has not chosen for me. It is the beauty of living in surrender.

Lest you believe that I'm over here living my best life in the perfect will of God, I want to make it clear that I'm not. Letting go does not come naturally to me, and I'm tempted to steal back control like anyone else.

> **When we are surrendered, we are re-ordering our lives so that everything revolves around and points to our Savior.**

The point I'm driving at is when I found surrender, God didn't ask me to give up a long list of things. He didn't say I was no longer allowed to date or go on vacation. I haven't, thus far, felt the Spirit guiding me to abandon all of my old friends and live a life of solitude. There has been no direct command to turn my entire life upside down and change everything. In fact, I feel more myself than I ever have in my forty-one years of life. When we are surrendered, we are re-ordering our lives so that everything revolves around and points to our Savior. Instead of trying to figure out how our earthly desires fit into what God wants for us, we find that the things of this world no longer hold value compared to what God can offer us. Our fulfillment is in God's promises and faithfulness, not our own ability to find ourselves.

Many of us spent our teens and twenties trying to figure out who we are. We made decisions that have been relatively insignificant in the grand scheme. And we made decisions that have had a lasting impact on our lives. Regardless of the outcome, our decisions were often our attempt at controlling our own destiny. This is what I refer to as "trying." We are doing everything under our own control. The idea of surrender is frightening because it requires us to let go of any control.

We spend an enormous amount of time "trying" different things in an attempt to determine what works best for our vision of our lives. I watch my students "try" things all the time. At the middle school level, it is usually a new makeup routine, a new group of friends, and even my patience (or

Trying is not the same as doing.

any adult's, for that matter.) Trying things out, seeking our own path, seems to be a hallmark of being human. Growing up I would alter existing cookie recipes, experiment with different ways to solve common problems, or try to figure out my future. It was always with *my* strength that I made these efforts. The end goal was solely for my own benefit.

Here's the thing with "trying"—it's usually just the minimum amount of effort required to appear as if we are accomplishing something in the direction of the original goal. Trying is not the same as doing. And we "try" for a lot of different reasons. A child "tries" to clean his room because he either doesn't want to or because he genuinely doesn't know where to start. An adult "tries" to save money because living within a budget is hard and uncomfortable. Generally speaking, when we use the word *try* it is because we need assistance of some sort. Before learning to trust God fully, I would *try* to read my Bible more or *try* to want to help people. It was always me "trying" on my own. After understanding surrender, I find myself not even trying. It looks more like, "God, I know I need to do this. I can't by myself. I need the Holy Spirit to take over. I'll mess it up. I need you. Move me. I'm asking that you will complete the work." I don't need to *try;* I need to *do.* The "do" in this case looks like accepting that I can't actually do it and then stepping aside so that God can work.

It takes effort to give up, doesn't it? It challenges our pride and creates a sense of unease when we realize giving up means not knowing the outcome. The thing is, we didn't really know the outcome to begin with. We think we can control the outcome if we control the input. But the painful reality is that short-term outcomes may be affected, and long-term outcomes are still very much unknown. What's crazy, though, is that the short-term outcomes actually *can* impact the long-term outcomes even though our input cannot guarantee the outcome. Are you still with me? Let me share some examples.

In Exodus, God sent Moses and Aaron to tell Pharaoh that they were getting ready to take God's people and peace out. As you can imagine, Pharaoh was a little hesitant to let his free labor go. Fortunately, God has no problem making a point through actions. Enter the plagues. (If you've never read about these directly in Scripture, I highly recommend it. Check out Exodus 7–11.) Moses and Aaron had to lead the Israelites away from Pharaoh, quickly, and in the middle of the night. Turns out, though, that Pharaoh was not ready to break up. Actually, upon closer inspection of the text I found out that God hardened Pharaoh's heart as a way to show his faithfulness to the people of Israel and remind the Israelites and the Egyptians exactly who our God was and is.

Then the LORD said to Moses, "Tell the Israelites to turn back and encamp near Pi Hahiroth, between Migdol and the sea. They are to encamp by the sea, directly opposite Baal Zephon. Pharaoh will think, 'The Israelites are wandering around the land in confusion, hemmed in by the desert.' And I will harden Pharaoh's heart, and he will pursue them. But I will gain glory for myself through Pharaoh and all his army, and the Egyptians will know that I am the LORD." So the Israelites did this.

When the king of Egypt was told that the people had fled, Pharaoh and his officials changed their minds about them and said, "What have we done? We have let the Israelites go and have lost their services!" So he had his chariot made ready and took his army with him. He took six hundred of the best chariots, along with all the other chariots of Egypt, with officers over all of them. The LORD hardened the heart of Pharaoh king of Egypt, so that he pursued the Israelites, who were marching out boldly. The Egyptians—all Pharaoh's horses and chariots, horsemen and troops—pursued the Israelites and overtook them as they camped by the sea near Pi Hahiroth, opposite Baal Zephon.

As Pharaoh approached, the Israelites looked up, and there were the Egyptians, marching after them. They were terrified and cried out to the LORD. They said to Moses, "Was it because there were no graves in Egypt that you brought us to the desert to die? What have you done to us by bringing us out of Egypt? Didn't we say to you in Egypt, 'Leave us alone; let us serve the Egyptians'? It would have been better for us to serve the Egyptians than to die in the desert!"

> Moses answered the people, "Do not be afraid. Stand firm and
> you will see the deliverance the LORD will bring you today. The
> Egyptians you see today you will never see again. The LORD will
> fight for you; you need only to be still." (Ex. 14:1–14)

Did anyone else catch that? These people were blessed in captiv-
ity by being able to multiply their numbers. God sent messengers
(Moses and Aaron) to pull them out of the depths of slavery. At
the time they could not stop praising God, vowing to worship
him all the days of their lives, and just generally letting him plan
all their next steps. All of the praise and gratitude lasted for . . .
three days. I'm not joking. They made it seventy-two hours (ac-
cording to our modern timetable) before falling apart and decid-
ing that they knew better than the Creator of the universe. God
was leading them with a pillar of cloud by day and a pillar of fire
by night. I mean, there was no question where they were to go.
And the moment they saw the Egyptians following, the moment
they thought they were in physical danger, the people began to
grumble and say slavery would have been better (vv. 10–12). Even
Moses faltered a little and asked for God to reveal the next part
of the plan.

Last year, when I read this for the for the first time (as an
adult who actually sought to glean something from the text),
something inside of me said, "You can't feel too bad about being
directionless when even the Israelites couldn't make themselves
follow God, who was physically in front of them." Granted,
it was the sarcastic, cynical part inside of me, but still. Think
about it. These people had not only two human leaders, but
the spirit of God in a visible cloud and fire. In front of them.
Directly guiding their path. And as soon as they saw some kind
of potential earthly danger, they were ready to go back into
slavery. SLAVERY.

That was the first time they grumbled on that journey. The second was not long after when they had escaped the Egyptian army who was pursuing them and experienced what is arguably one of the greatest miracles of all time - the parting of the Red Sea. The full details of that rescue can be found in Exodus 14. When we look at Exodus 15 we see round two of complaining when the Israelites, after traveling without water for three days, arrive at Marah to find that the water is bitter and unsuitable for drinking. They immediately begin griping. God, once again, provides a way for the water to be cleaned. Not long after, God lays out the plan for manna and quail to be provided daily. Will the mumbling and grumbling stop once this plan is in place? No. And it's shocking to me because all needs are being met.

Big leap here—that's like my guinea pig waking up one day and refusing to eat the dry hay and water I've provided because she was tired of it. She's the only one who would be hurt by that plan of attack. I don't even like her that much (don't ask), and I'm still willing to provide for her. Meanwhile, God loves us more than we could ever possibly imagine, and the Israelites had

> **I'm raising my hand. It's me. I'm one of those dummies.**

determined that they knew more and had the right to complain about what was being provided. It's nuts—those dummies.

This is when I just go ahead and look in the mirror while I'm talking about "those dummies." I'm raising my hand. It's me. I'm one of those dummies.

We are not actually dummies, though. We are sinful people so desperately in need of a Savior. The more I think about the Israelites and the beginning of the wandering, the more I recognize how humans have never changed. There is something about *those* people that touches a part deep inside my soul because it's not *those* people; it's just *people*. It's us.

If I am they and they are I, then somewhere tucked into the lines of their stories there must be a place for my story. And your story. This was a lightbulb moment for me. If the life I'm living is a reflection of the lives that were lived on the pages of my Bible, I want to know more! I want to see how the Israelites handled themselves and each other because it is directly related to how I handle myself and others. What if I'm able to learn from their mistakes? What if God has something to teach me in 2023 AD by showing me what happened in 1300 BC?

> **Author Suggestion: Take a moment to think about where you are in life right now. Are you wandering? Are you enjoying the promised land? Are you wondering what's next? Pray. Right now. Ask God what he wants you to learn through his Word. Ask him to open your eyes, your heart, your mind to the possibility that he has given you direction in his ancient text. Open your Bible to Exodus and read a chapter. Tomorrow, read another chapter. The next day, read another chapter. It's in there. Read.*

Chapter 3

A Rescue Story

Planning, planning, planning. Humans always need a plan. We lay out our clothes the night before, make grocery lists, calculate which parent will take which kid to which practice, and so on. As a teacher, I have to plan every moment with my students, or chaos ensues. Some of us have programmed ourselves to over-plan to maintain an illusion of control.

Believers can even fall into a trap of planning when and where to share the gospel. Oof. We make a plan to help at vacation Bible school, sign up to teach Sunday school, and spend a year preparing for a two-week mission trip. But outside of those times, who are we sharing Jesus with? Are we even talking about Jesus when it's not prearranged? Are we even thinking about Jesus?

Coordinating and scheduling are not inherently wrong practices. We are called to be good stewards of our time (Ps. 90:12; Eph. 5:15–17). But what happens when we become

> **Believers can even fall into a trap of planning when and where to share the gospel.**

engulfed in our plans to the point that God's plan is completely snuffed out? Are we listening to God's plan for us or expecting him to bless our plan for ourselves?

Much like the Israelites who wandered for forty years (Ex. 16—Josh. 1), in my previous life I would be in awe of God's provision then turn away from his plan to follow my own. I would cry out when I thought I needed some earthly direction or gift, and then I'd promptly forget God's faithfulness a short while later.

"What college should I attend?"

"Which job should I choose?"

"Help me get over this breakup."

"Please let her be okay."

"I know you can do _____; let me be the one who gets that blessing."

The list goes on.

Now that I reside in the promised land, I see the fault in my prayer logic during the wilderness season of my life. Not only was I solely going to God for requests that were oddly specific to circumstances I could control, I very often would present God with the options I had already vetted so he would have some direction. The absurdity of my prayer life before surrender was truly something to behold.

But we all do this, don't we? We research the schools we want to attend; we use logic to figure out the top three choices; we apply only to those schools, then we pray that God would tell us which one he would like us to go to. And don't forget that we add requirements to his choice, such as: "Make it clear by providing funding. Please and thank you." It gets even crazier. We justify all of these prayers by telling ourselves that our pursuit is noble and sound, so obviously God would agree that we are placing the correct options in front of him. Whaaaaaat?!

Replace that example with the last request you placed before God. Was it a job? A name for the new baby? A school for your child? Where to serve at church? (Anyone else feel that gut punch with the last one? Yikes.)

Since this type of prayer—the "planning my path then asking God to bless it" type—was not modeled for me at home, I must assume that I picked it up based on cultural influences. My parents only spoke of allowing the Holy Spirit to lead and reading my Bible daily. They are imperfect, but I can't say they were wrong about these truths. I grew up watching the hand of God on our family, and still, I wandered. If nothing else gives you hope in your story, I pray you will hear what I just said. I had every single advantage regarding spiritual life and maturity, and still I wandered. Not because God doesn't love me, or my parents got something wrong, or because Satan had it out for me from the beginning. I wandered because we live in a broken world, and we are broken people. I'm in the promised land because God is faithful, his timing is perfect, and he has throughout my life made beauty from the ashes I laid at his feet (Is. 61:3).

> **I had every single advantage regarding spiritual life and maturity, and still I wandered.**

Until we have learned how to surrender—truly surrender in a way that not only lets go of control but flat-out refuses to take control—we will never fully enjoy the peace that passes all understanding (Phil. 4:7). It is a peace that demands our surrender and overwhelms our senses in the best ways possible. It encompasses our heart and soul in a manner that protects and heals all at the same time. One moment of that breathtaking, life-giving, remarkable peace could convince even the most adamant heathen that God exists and is worth pursuing. And to attain it, we need only open our hands and let go of the earthly things we have come to rely on.

Even still, I get it wrong at least fifty percent of the time. And by *wrong* I mean I have difficulty surrendering. I find it most challenging regarding how I spend my time. Am I investing in a TV series with no biblical value? Am I investing time teaching my daughter or just watching a movie with her? Am I investing in another vacation because I just need to get away? What exactly are the returns on my investments? Are those returns building my kingdom or building the kingdom of God?

As I ponder these questions, I have ideas like tracking my time for a week to see where it's going or immediately cutting out television. The problem with these thoughts is that they come from a wholly human perspective that seeks to fix the underlying issue on my own. Even if I rearrange my calendar to eliminate television, work with my child in the kitchen, and feed the homeless, it will all be in vain. When it comes

> **Giving up on choosing our own direction is what leads to surrender.**

down to it, there is no to-do list for surrender. Obviously, we can make choices that are more God-honoring. Obviously, we can take steps toward understanding God instead of walking away. Obviously, these are not evil pursuits. And obviously, others who see these actions will be in awe of our spirituality and good discipline. (That last thought always gets me because . . . well . . . pride is an all too common sin for me. A sin which has presented itself throughout the generations of my family. My dad recognized deep pride in his life, pointed it out in my life, and I now watch it in the actions of my daughter.) If we dig deeper, we know that our actions are not what create a heart of surrender. Giving up on choosing our own direction is what leads to surrender. Read that again.

This whole conundrum reminds me of a study we did at my church in the book of Romans a few years ago. Paul teaches that we do not love God more because we follow his commands; instead, we follow his commands as an outpouring of how much we love him. Let's back up and set the stage a bit better. This is all found in the New Testament (the second half of the Bible), so it requires us to step out of wandering toward the promised land (Old Testament; the front half of the Bible). Stay with me.

There was this guy named Saul who indeed found his purpose in life. He was incredibly gifted and passionate about persecuting Christians. At every opportunity (many self-created), Saul would publicly abuse followers of the early church. Here is how his actions are recounted in the Bible:

And Saul approved of their killing him.

On that day a great persecution broke out against the church in Jerusalem, and all except the apostles were scattered throughout Judea and Samaria. Godly men buried Stephen and mourned deeply for him. But Saul began to destroy the church. Going from house to house, he dragged off both men and women and put them in prison . . .

Meanwhile, Saul was still breathing out murderous threats against the Lord's disciples. He went to the high priest and asked him for letters to the synagogues in Damascus, so that if he found any there who belonged to the Way, whether men or women, he might take them as prisoners to Jerusalem. (Acts 8:1–3; 9:1–2)

Being born and bred in a Christian household means I've read, heard, re-read, and re-heard the story of Saul's conversion countless times over forty-one years. Like most Bible stories, children get the gist of what happened, and as we age, we are encouraged to inspect everything thoroughly and then apply it to our lives. And then, for our remaining years here on earth, we hear sermon after sermon on the same stories, each trying to find a different angle to reach the congregation and spark a new passion for hearing about Jesus. That's all well and good. I'm not opposed to it. But I never knew how powerful the Word of God can be when I explore it for myself.

Saul perhaps did not understand that honoring God was about a relationship and not just the rules. When I read about Saul as an adult, a few things come to mind. The first being that I have often been a Saul quite possibly in more ways than I care to admit. I've held my position as VBS director as some type of medal of honor that should help me compete for Christian of the Year. I have held myself in high regard because I was at church every time the doors opened, and even at one point, was given a key to the building, spending many hours there alone preparing for various events. Exhausted from trying so hard to win some cosmic competition and frustrated that I still felt like something was missing, I eventually gave up on being the traditional churchgoer and decided to start judging them instead. Much like the old adage, "If you can't beat 'em, join 'em," I lived this truth: if beating them doesn't bring satisfaction, mock them. Saul's version involved brutal abuse, but still, Saul and I have common ground.

The second truth I took away from Saul's story is that he held so tightly to what he believed was right that he left destruction in his wake. Imagine a world in which you simply seek to destroy the lives of anyone who disagrees with you and is willing to admit it publicly. Slowly I began to realize that my form of destruction was ruined relationships and missed opportunities to share the gospel. Maybe I didn't publicly criticize or even throw those who oppose me in jail. But I have avoided difficult situations and conversations. I've abandoned friendships. And I have sullied the very name of Jesus by simply being reckless with my words and actions because being loving meant living through the messy bits. The messy bits take time and patience— two things I do not have an abundance of on my own. No one really likes the messy bits because they're uncomfortable. I don't like discomfort.

Saul was chasing righteousness. I was chasing righteousness. He was pursuing, I assume, his own version of perfection. I was also pursuing what I believed to be the perfect Christian life. Saul was getting it wrong. And so was I. The good news is that God chose both of us. There is nothing Saul or I could have done apart from just wander through existence completely lifeless. Our common ground was that the Savior of the world chose to breathe new life into us. Thankfully, Saul and I share the best common ground that can be found on this side of heaven—our rescue story.

As he neared Damascus on his journey, suddenly a light from heaven flashed around him. He fell to the ground and heard a voice say to him, "Saul, Saul, why do you persecute me?"

"Who are you, Lord?" Saul asked.

"I am Jesus, whom you are persecuting," he replied. "Now get up and go into the city, and you will be told what you must do."

The men traveling with Saul stood there speechless; they heard the sound but did not see anyone. Saul got up from the ground, but when he opened his eyes he could see nothing. So they led him by the hand into Damascus. For three days he was blind, and did not eat or drink anything.

In Damascus there was a disciple named Ananias. The Lord called to him in a vision, "Ananias!"

"Yes, Lord," he answered.

The Lord told him, "Go to the house of Judas on Straight Street and ask for a man from Tarsus named Saul, for he is praying. In a vision he has seen a man named Ananias come and place his hands on him to restore his sight."

"Lord," Ananias answered, "I have heard many reports about this man and all the harm he has done to your holy people in Jerusalem. And he has come here with authority from the chief priests to arrest all who call on your name."

But the Lord said to Ananias, "Go! This man is my chosen instrument to proclaim my name to the Gentiles and their kings and to the people of Israel. I will show him how much he must suffer for my name."

Then Ananias went to the house and entered it. Placing his hands on Saul, he said, "Brother Saul, the Lord—Jesus, who appeared to you on the road as you were coming here—has sent me so that you may see again and be filled with the Holy Spirit." Immediately, something like scales fell from Saul's eyes, and he could see again. He got up and was baptized, and after taking some food, he regained his strength. (Acts 9:3–19)

What do you say after reading something like that? For a good portion of my life I was completely unaffected except that it was a cool way to get someone's attention. There were people I'd like to blind with a bright light. Other than that, it was just another story. For a brief period there was a part of me that felt it unfair for Saul to be forced into surrender and then get celebrated as if he had done something. This man got to change his name and become a whole new person. I got to document the date of my salvation prayer in the front cover of my Bible. Not quite the same. And then I began to wonder why it wasn't the same. Why did I hear these amazing salvation stories and mine was so bland? Did I do something wrong? Was my life just a little too whitewashed? Something was definitely amiss.

The good news is that Saul and I actually *did* accept the same good news. Not only do our sins against our heavenly Father share a few details, but our surrender stories do as well. Before you ask, no I was not physically blinded by a bright light while walking out of the Starbucks one day. But my sins were just as heinous in God's eyes, and God reached down and rescued me the same way he reached down and rescued Saul. It was just that fast. In hindsight, that moment has completely changed my life, and I now want the world to hear about how incredible the rest of our days on earth can be if we choose to live completely surrendered.

I began this chapter by talking about God's plan instead of our own. Let's revisit that idea for a minute. First, we are all like Saul in some way. Our sins are just as dirty and damaging as his—and anyone else's when it comes down to it. Second, our plans don't matter! They truly don't. We can be asking God to bless our college choice, our next car purchase, a job transition, or a new role at church, and none of it matters (Phil. 3:7–8). It is all for naught if we are not doing it for the purpose of sharing Christ with others.

Anyone who calls themselves a child of God has a rescue story. We cannot save ourselves. We do not make the decision to follow Christ. We are dead in our sin, wandering this earth with no purpose until Christ picks us up and breathes new life into us. Once that takes place, once we claim victory in Jesus or acknowledge his forgiveness and grace, a rescue story has been written. If we fail to share our rescue with others or tuck it away until Sunday morning rolls around then our efforts, our plans, our decisions will all be in vain. Nothing matters if it is not done with the intent to surrender our plans to God.

Does your job seem pointless? Do you want a way out because your co-workers are relentlessly absurd? Ask yourself these questions: Do I have a rescue story to share? Have I shared it? Am I living it?

Are you struggling in your marriage? Is your spouse not serving your needs? Ask yourself these questions: Do I have a rescue story to share? Have I shared it? Am I living it?

Should I buy this car from this dealership? Is it the right purchase? Ask yourself these questions: Do I have a rescue story to share? Have I shared it? Am I living it?

Quite honestly, if we don't have a rescue story or we're not living in the beauty of our rescue story, then why bother with anything else? We are not simply talking about a prayer that involves A (Admit I'm a sinner), B (Believe Jesus died for my sins on the cross), and C (Confess my sins and ask Jesus into my heart). That is the *most* important step in your life, and it brings salvation. Bar none. Do that *first*. But once you've done that part, what comes next? The rest of your days. All of them. The Mondays and Tuesdays and Wednesdays. What happens during *those* hours, weeks, and months? We don't get re-saved every day. We *surrender* every day.

Think of it like this. We make a decision to get married. We spend time planning, the big day arrives, and a huge party is thrown in our honor. We do not then re-plan and re-party each of the remaining days of the marriage. No. What follows the wedding is a lifelong commitment to serve our spouse each day. And that is messy and complicated, and we make lots of mistakes. But, we wake up each day with the intention of doing our best to serve our spouse. Some days it's really difficult because serving does not line up with what we actually want to do. Some days it's really easy (usually when the spouse is on a beach trip with their friends). In a healthy marriage, we are proud to introduce our spouse or happy to tell people we are married. Our decisions revolve around shared goals and responsibilities. This is what a healthy marriage looks like.

In my limited experience, a healthy relationship with God looks very similar. Not exactly the same because no spouse is perfect nor are we commanded to worship our spouse. However, we have the moment of salvation (the wedding) and then the cheers and excitement fade away. What comes next? It's not supposed to be a one and done type of event. It's a lifelong commitment to serve God. How can we serve him fully if we are not surrendered?

For me, that healthy relationship part didn't start until last year. After thirty-two years of being saved God brought me to a place of surrender and brought my rescue story full circle. There are probably numerous reasons why it happened thirty-two years later. I'm sure most of them involve my being stubborn and prideful. But I'm here now. The question is, what will I do with it? Am I living in it every day? Am I asking for a heart of surrender and confessing sin as soon as it happens? Do those around me see a difference?

> **Author Suggestion: For you, the question begins with whether or not you have accepted Christ as your Savior. Have you confessed to him that you know you're a sinner and need his redeeming grace? If not, then start there. (Then email me so I can celebrate with you! author.sabrina.faubel@gmail.com) In the days following that, ask for clear vision and for the Holy Spirit to fill you. If you have accepted salvation, then ask yourself if you know how powerful your rescue story is. Can you point to a specific time when surrender was no doubt what you started living in every day?. Let God know where your heart is and that you want to let him lead.*

Chapter 4

Trust and Obey

Can you imagine the pieces of a giant floor puzzle falling from the sky and dropping into the correct place on earth in such a way that each section clicks together in perfect harmony? This is what I imagine the bird's-eye view of my life looks like. The pieces are dropping from the sky, beautifully making their descent with a clear destination. As each one softly hits the ground and begins to nuzzle into its perfect position, I can almost hear the angels softly humming their hallelujahs.

And there I am. Running from piece to piece, laboring away to change its position to match the pieces that have already landed. I am pushing, pulling, and lifting the corners to match everything up. In some scenes, I'm even quietly trying to change the shape by shaving off the edges, taking shortcuts. In the bottom left corner is an area where I decided I liked someone else's puzzle better so I repainted my pieces to try to look like theirs. When the new pieces don't seem to match the old pieces, I begin trying to change the old pieces. All of my efforts are futile, of course.

At this point, any logical person is asking, "If the pieces were already falling into their perfect position, why are you trying so hard to change them?" Great question.

Currently, I'm reading through Deuteronomy, I can't help but ask the same question of the Israelites. If you've ever taken a gander at this particular part of the Old Testament you know that it is a book of repeating. I'm not sure if that's a theologically sound statement. I'm a novice when it comes to studying the Bible so I feel confident that all I can do is call it as I see it. Because I have already read Genesis through Numbers, I know that Deuteronomy is mostly about reminding God's people (the Israelites) about all of the rules and regulations he gave to Moses about forty years prior. More importantly, in my mind, it's a reminder of God's faithfulness to the Israelites. It bears repeating.

Are we all familiar with *why* the Israelites had to wander for forty years? Because every time God lovingly dropped a puzzle piece into place, his own people whom he had delivered from slavery and consistently provided for —kept shifting and changing the pieces to fit their image of what the future needed to look like. And oftentimes, it wasn't even what they thought the future should look like. It was what they thought the present should look like. It is mind-numbingly ridiculous how they could possibly complain when their life was so simple. Be free. Be free from slavery. Be free from providing for yourself. Be free from stressing over what direction to take. A good and perfect God is right there with you. But they wanted a different puzzle.

They got frustrated. They got confused. They tried to morph God's perfect puzzle into a picture that matched what they created in their (sinful) mind's eye. This is strange to many of us because we have read about how God led the Israelites via Moses and Aaron. The text clearly states that God provided food and direction. How can such a simple task like following a pillar of cloud by day and a pillar of fire by night go so terribly wrong?

I heard Pastor Bryan Loritts once explain it using one word: *disappointment.* He said that because the Israelites did not feel as if God was meeting their expectations, what they were met with instead was disappointment—disappointment in God's availability. They had an expectation of hearing from God on a regular basis. When Moses had been away for a long period and they did not have that communication, their faith faltered and their expectations were crushed. It was a powerful message because it pointed out yet another way in which *my* journey and that of the people from an ancient time are not that different. Countless times I have

> **And countless times I have taken matters into my own hands because I was too impatient to wait on God's provision.**

been frustrated by not hearing from God. And countless times I have taken matters into my own hands because I was too impatient to wait on God's provision.

Let's take a peek at what the Bible has to say in Exodus 16.

> When the dew was gone, thin flakes like frost on the ground appeared on the desert floor. When the Israelites saw it, they said to each other, "What is it?" For they did not know what it was.
>
> Moses said to them, "It is the bread the LORD has given you to eat. This is what the LORD has commanded: 'Everyone is to gather as much as they need. Take an omer for each person you have in your tent.'"
>
> The Israelites did as they were told; some gathered much, some little. And when they measured it by the omer, the one who gathered much did not have too much, and the one who

gathered little did not have too little. Everyone had gathered just as much as they needed.

Then Moses said to them, "No one is to keep any of it until morning."

However, some of them paid no attention to Moses; they kept part of it until morning, but it was full of maggots and began to smell. So Moses was angry with them.

Each morning everyone gathered as much as they needed, and when the sun grew hot, it melted away. On the sixth day, they gathered twice as much—two omers for each person—and the leaders of the community came and reported this to Moses. He said to them, "This is what the LORD commanded: 'Tomorrow is to be a day of sabbath rest, a holy sabbath to the LORD. So bake what you want to bake and boil what you want to boil. Save whatever is left and keep it until morning.'"

So they saved it until morning, as Moses commanded, and it did not stink or get maggots in it. "Eat it today," Moses said, "because today is a sabbath to the LORD. You will not find any of it on the ground today. Six days you are to gather it, but on the seventh day, the Sabbath, there will not be any."

Nevertheless, some of the people went out on the seventh day to gather it, but they found none. Then the LORD said to Moses, "How long will you refuse to keep my commands and my instructions? Bear in mind that the LORD has given you the Sabbath; that is why on the sixth day he gives you bread for two days. Everyone is to stay where they are on the seventh day; no one is to go out." So the people rested on the seventh day.

The people of Israel called the bread manna. It was white like coriander seed and tasted like wafers made with honey. Moses said, "This is what the LORD has commanded: 'Take an omer of manna and keep it for the generations to come, so they can see the bread I gave you to eat in the wilderness when I brought you out of Egypt.'"

So Moses said to Aaron, "Take a jar and put an omer of manna in it. Then place it before the LORD to be kept for the generations to come."

As the LORD commanded Moses, Aaron put the manna with the tablets of the covenant law, so that it might be preserved. The Israelites ate manna forty years, until they came to a land that was settled; they ate manna until they reached the border of Canaan. (Ex. 16:14–35)

Daily bread was literally falling from the sky. Hungry? Here you go. Take this perfect nourishment. There's only one condition. I need you to take only enough for the day ahead. Don't overcomplicate your life. Don't carry more than you need for today. Don't plan ahead. Trust that I'll be here tomorrow to take care of you. God was leading his children in an exercise of obedience and trust.

One of the songs I remember from youth choir is a spritely tune set to a Southern Baptist-appropriate level of steel drum music for a Sunday morning. It was the words to an old hymn I remembered from childhood, but with a more upbeat tempo. "Trust. Trust and obey, for there's no other way to be happy in Jesus but to trust and obey." If that song doesn't exemplify the life lessons God was trying to teach the Israelites in the wilderness, I don't know what does.

In the words of that memorable melody I find comfort and a challenge. It sounds incredibly easy to just rest and allow the God of the universe to direct my path. In fact, it sounds downright amazing and relaxing until it means that I don't get to know the outcome. I'm not privy to the exact destination. I'm not even allowed to put the address in Google Maps, much less watch the car avatar follow the blue route. The best place for me is in the backseat with my eyes closed. In this case, the best place is the most uncomfortable place. It is the place where I must surrender all control and authority. It is the place where I should be seen and not heard, which is counterintuitive in today's culture. Though I suppose it is also counterintuitive these days to fully trust something outside of ourselves. God calls us to do both if we want to live life more abundantly.

Once in a while, I imagine God as a puzzle maker. Puzzle pieces look really confusing at first. They have a few common shapes, but the picture on each one is only going to match one part of the puzzle. Even if I were to find two pieces whose shapes are shockingly similar (or identical), the illustration on each would be different. Where they fit within the puzzle would be different. No two pieces of the same puzzle can look the same because it would negate the need for one of them. He has crafted beautiful pieces of artwork, carefully cut each piece to fit together, and started the process of building each individual work with a love that only a puzzle maker could provide.

And then there's me. Down here on earth trying desperately to figure out which pieces go where and what my puzzle will look like when it's all finished. I get impatient in a season of singleness and start trying to make a piece from a relationship fit in the section of the puzzle designed to look like the single life. I don't want to wait for the grief phase to run its course so instead I start trying to put together the part of the puzzle where I've moved on. The puzzle I try to create has a bunch of gaps and holes. I'm tired of waiting for one part to come together so I quickly dart over to another corner and start building something there. All the while God is lovingly creating new pieces to fill in the gaps and holes I've left behind.

When surrender started to take hold in my life, so many things were revealed that I had not recognized earlier. Gaping spaces in my puzzle were filled because I stopped and waited long enough to watch God work instead of trying to work everything out for myself. Places where I had moved on because the lesson was just too hard were the same places that God was giving me yet another chance to learn something I would need to know. Tiny shards of my broken heart were being healed and shaped into a more beautiful heart than I ever had before. The puzzle heart I had created for myself was lopsided and the color had faded. God restored those old puzzle pieces in the same way a restoration artist would obsess over restoring a Rembrandt that had been burned in a fire.

Each of us *is* a priceless work of art. And the pieces do not have to be perfect in order for us to go before God and surrender to his will. I would argue that the opposite is true. The more gaps and holes (i.e., shame and sin), the more room we have to watch him do incredible things in our lives. It's also good to note that sin, no matter the size, creates separation from God and structural issues in our puzzles. Lying to our teacher about why our homework is not done is sin in the same way lying to our spouse about where we've been is sin. Yes, the earthly consequences are going to most likely be greater for one than the other. Yes, our shame or guilt will be greater for one than the other. But sin separates us from God, no matter how great or small the earthly ramifications. Any sin, on any given day, for any reason, separates us from God.

> **The puzzle heart I had created for myself was lopsided and the color had faded.**

Your puzzle is your own. Are you allowing God to place the pieces, or are you stubbornly holding onto your pieces so you can place them where you want within your chosen timeframe? Are you accepting the pieces God is placing in front of you and trusting that he knows which piece will fall next, or are you insistent that the border must be complete before you work on the inside? Surrender will look different for each of us because we each have our own unique puzzle to work out. Just remember that your story is powerful. It doesn't matter if God has filled holes the size of entire pieces or if he has made minor reconstructions here and there. Other people who are busy building their own masterpiece need to hear about your Puzzler and why you chose for it to be God instead of you.

> *Author Suggestion: It is not often that we have an opportunity to share all of our puzzle pieces with another person. Instead, maybe we should just start with a single piece and how God placed it or what you learned from trying to place it yourself. If you cannot think of a place where God was faithful or you don't feel #blessed today, maybe it's because you're placing your own pieces much too often. It's okay to let God do the work. Spend a moment in prayer, asking God to reveal what percentage of the process is you and what percentage is him.*

Chapter 5

Coffee-Ground Faith

Most people are familiar with the idea of faith the size of a mustard seed. Even if you haven't read the Bible, you've most likely heard this reference at some point in your life. It comes from Matthew 17 in the New Testament.

> When they came to the crowd, a man approached Jesus and knelt before him. "Lord, have mercy on my son," he said. "He has seizures and is suffering greatly. He often falls into the fire or into the water. I brought him to your disciples, but they could not heal him."
>
> "You unbelieving and perverse generation," Jesus replied, "how long shall I stay with you? How long shall I put up with you? Bring the boy here to me." Jesus rebuked the demon, and it came out of the boy, and he was healed at that moment.
>
> Then the disciples came to Jesus in private and asked, "Why couldn't we drive it out?" He replied, "Because you have so little faith. Truly I tell you, if you have faith as small as a mustard seed, you can say to this mountain, 'Move from here to there,' and it will move. Nothing will be impossible for you." (Matt. 17:14–20)

If you're reading this entire passage for the first time, it might surprise you like it did me. This is not the calm, patient Jesus that I envision when I think of New Testament stories. I'm no theologian, but there is obviously a general understanding that Jesus was the embodiment of peace, love, and joy. In this particular story however, we see Jesus calling out the disciples for their lack of faith. I could be reading it wrong, but this is what I hear or imagine when I read verse 17: "Are you kidding me? Did we not just go over this, you guys? Seriously. Were you not taking notes when I told you that I was giving you the power to cast out demons? You know I'm not going to be around forever to clean up your messes. Father, could you talk to them? Clearly, I'm not explaining things correctly! Good grief!" I pray that my interpretation is not blasphemous. Like I said, I'm not a Bible scholar. I'm a divorced, middle-aged woman who belongs to the Most High King just trying to make sense of the directions he left for me.

Can you imagine being a literal follower of Christ—as in, physically following Jesus around town—and still not having faith the size of a mustard seed? It seems like that would be akin to assisting a surgeon every day and still not knowing whether to hand over the scalpel or the forceps. It's a mustard seed, for crying out loud! My understanding is that "the size of a mustard seed" was used as a proverbial saying to mean the smallest amount of something. Jesus is telling the disciples that even the smallest amount of faith could have brought about healing for the boy. And it seems to me that Jesus is also calling attention to the fact that he will not be with the disciples forever. They need to understand the power that has been given to them because in the not so distant future that faith, and the indwelling of the Holy Spirit, is all they will have, as Jesus will no longer be directly in front of them.

This is where the Bible gets very real for me. My dad was an amazing human and was the epitome of a godly man in my life. It would be ridiculous to compare my father to Jesus, but as far as a real, tangible example that existed in my life to guide me in a Christ-like fashion, my dad fits the bill. My entire life I read about the disciples having to watch Jesus die on the cross and feeling the pain of his absence. But I never understood that loss until I had to walk the earth without my dad. It was utter confusion and chaos in my heart that eventually led me to the greatest gift my dad could

This is where the Bible gets very real for me.

have ever left me—an understanding of surrendering my life to God and the freedom that comes with it.

Dad passed on a Monday in May. My daughter and I had arrived at my parent's home for dinner. We were a few minutes earlier than expected. When we walked in the door I peeked back into Dad's room, and he was finding the strength to get ready to join us at the table. About fifteen minutes later Mom went to check on him and yelled for me in a panicked tone. I already knew what had happened.

In hindsight, I'm very thankful that Mom did not go through that alone. I'm thankful for when it happened as I had just finished my second semester of grad school so I was starting a three-week break before summer classes. And I'm thankful that Dad left us at a time when he was still able to care for himself, which he had always expressed that he would prefer.

I walked around in a haze for the first month as the school year wound down, we handled estate things, and I adjusted to the enormous hole that now existed in my heart and my life. I cried every day and couldn't make myself eat a thing. That's really saying something because I'm an eater. Never in my life have I experienced a loss of appetite—*never*. I made it through month one and headed into summer having canceled all existing plans because it just seemed like too much to pack, get in the car, and go somewhere. I wanted to be sad.

I've learned that, much like divorce, the loss of a parent is not something people outside of the survival circle can understand with any accuracy. As a church body we don't do a very good job of letting people be sad. Everyone wants to put a positive spin on things and make the world comfortable again. Can we all just agree that growth occurs in the uncomfortable places and then collectively walk silently beside people who are in uncomfortable places? (Asking for a friend).

> ## As a church body we don't do a very good job of letting people be sad.

Leaving my house even to buy groceries was a chore that summer. I thought I was handling grief so well because I was continuing with grad school and managing to do laundry every week. The crying continued but became more sporadic and less intense, so I assumed I was truly moving through the grief process at an astounding rate. But sometimes in our rush to be over the hard stuff, we miss the beauty of being under the weight of it. The alternative, however, is to sit in our grief, sit in our failed relationship, sit in a particularly frustrating season, sit in a job we don't like. But that alternative does not fit our narrative of how life is supposed to be. And this is when we seek to maintain control instead of pulling together mustard-seed faith and giving up control to our Creator.

At the end of that summer I was at my heaviest weight ever and struggling to be on my feet for more than an hour at a time. (Clearly, I had rediscovered my appetite somewhere between June and August.) My being a middle school teacher, that lack of energy and ability to be on my feet would not bode well for me with what would end up being my toughest year yet, ahead of me. To add to the pressure, my finances had gotten quite messy, and I now felt the weight of not asking my parents for help preemptively, when I had the chance. I didn't necessarily need it at that time, but my parents were always the backup plan. There was something oddly unsettling now about needing to ask my mom for financial help when she was already trying to manage everything on her own following the loss of her spouse of fifty years. I needed to face the fact that I was now my own backup plan.

At some point during the summer I had decided to pick up my First 5 app every day and spend at least fifteen minutes reading and praying. Let me tell you, fifteen minutes was a whole lot in the beginning. Consistency had never been a strength of mine, and so my attendance at these self-appointed morning meetings was sketchy at best. (Sidenote: First 5 is a product of Proverbs 31 Ministries. First 5 is a *free* app that gives access to a boatload of Bible study plans, each one taking approximately ten to fifteen minutes to read through. It is worth checking out.)

By the end of August I was reading and praying every single morning, first thing. The school year started, and, as expected, it was a humdinger

And just like that, God picked me up and carried me into the promised land.

with no respite in sight. By week two I was sitting on my couch at 5:30 a.m., reading my app and praying. About two words into that prayer I started crying unexplainably. And all I could manage to do was repeat the words, "I need you," over and over—in my head and out loud. And just like that, God picked me up and carried me into the promised land.

I don't know what day of the week it was or the specific date on the calendar. There was no emotional worship song or an altar call. In that moment I honestly did not even know the extent of what was happening. I felt nothing apart from my utter inability to exist another second on this earth without the Holy Spirit taking control. I don't even think it was mustard-seed faith. I'm pretty sure it was more like coffee-ground faith. Probably even used coffee grounds. The yucky part that you trash after it's been soaked in steaming hot water and then all of the good parts have drained away. It's all I had left. It's all I had to give. And that's all it took.

> *Author Suggestion: Stop. Think about your coffee ground moment. Consider the astonishing way God stepped in to pick you up. If you don't have a coffee ground moment - that's ok. Take a moment to organize your thoughts around ways God has been faithful to you. If you're not sure you believe in God - that's ok, too. Take a moment to ask yourself "What if this is true?"*

Chapter 6

Slippery Slopes and Sin Seeds

I'm not a marketing genius, so it is with awe that I think back on one particular item from my childhood. How could a company make money from selling a long, thin vinyl shower curtain with a banana-shaped sprinkler head made of cheap plastic? It *had* to be expert marketing. For $9.95, a family could own summer happiness in a box. I don't know if it was the simplicity of setup or the lack of space needed for storage, but the world went crazy over the invention of the Slip 'N Slide. The commercials (yes, TV advertisements were a thing) showed kids of all ages having the time of their lives, throwing themselves onto the hard ground and getting covered in water. It looked like a makeshift water park in your backyard.

Our family owned one of these gems. And we fortunately had a hill on the side of our house, so the belly-flopping at high speeds was kept to a minimum. Gravity was kind to us. I remember the setup process and the re-setup process when the end of the slide was creating a mud pile fit for the prodigal son and his pigs.

If memory serves me correctly, the re-setup process took place reasonably often because, well, a constant stream of water from the hose is bound to oversaturate any lawn.

As an adult, I think of the parallels between the Slip 'N Slide from childhood and the many sin-filled slippery slopes I've traversed over the years. The critical elements of my favorite childhood toy include setup, fun, re-set up, slightly less fun (as we become covered in grass and mud), and eventually a cleanup process that involves putting away the toy and washing off from head to toe. Metaphorical slippery slopes follow an almost identical pattern.

The symbolic version usually begins with a great idea. It doesn't have to be a complicated idea. We could refer to it as a seed. In fact, the simpler the idea, the bigger the temptation. Or, the smaller the seed, the bigger the weed. We convince ourselves that it's so tiny it won't matter. It's a new job with an extra hour commute that pays more money, a few songs on the radio that celebrate sinful habits, a movie that promotes a sinful lifestyle, or a television show that glorifies things that God hates. All of these are such tiny, insignificant parts of our day-to-day life. And yet . . . they are often the setup. These are moments when we choose the world instead of God. We allow the tiny seed to be planted in the depths of our souls. These are moments when we convince ourselves that we are just an outside spectator; it doesn't make a difference because we read our Bible, pray often, and go to church every Sunday. The fact is that we cannot live holy lives and be passively living like the world. It flat-out won't work. Not even a little. We must choose a side of the proverbial fence. If we do not, the magnet on the worldly side will pull us toward it. It is a never-ending battle for

> **Or, the smaller the seed, the bigger the weed.**

our righteousness. We are either actively pursuing God or passively pursuing the world.

I could argue that these things are not good for us because that time could be spent on more godly pursuits. I could say that we need to refocus our attention on God, and then we won't care about those things anymore. I could even submit to you that as long as we spend MORE time on God, the earthly things don't matter as much. Also, as long as you don't do those things around other people or your children, then you're only impacting yourself. And, of course, you can handle the delicate balance of being *in* the world and not *of* it. Right?

Herein lies our problem. We are sheep. To our very core, we are sheep. Do you remember what sheep are? The dumbest animals on the face of

> **And the whole point for us is to follow God day by day.**

the earth. We will follow wolves as if they were shepherds because we cannot care for ourselves. Sheep need a shepherd. Full stop. There is no way around that fact. And with every step of wandering, we move away from the Good Shepherd and toward the wolf shepherd. Pastures are not all flat, safely manicured terrain where we can peruse freely without concern for danger. We live in an inherently treacherous pasture with wooded areas, watering holes that can drown us, hills and valleys, and even rocky paths.

The Israelites faced similar terrain while traveling in the wilderness. I often think about this and reassure myself I'm in good company. They still made it to the promised land . . . and so did I. But it is only through God's never-ending love and mercy that any of us were able to reach our God-ordained destination. I think that's what gets sticky about surrender. We can't *think* or *act* our way into it. By nature, it is something that does not come with a checklist or specific directions. The whole point for the Israelites was to follow God day by day. And the whole point for us is to follow God day by day.

I am a people observer (which I think sounds much less creepy than "people watcher"). While I am known to proclaim the occasional judgment of a fifty-something lady walking into Torrid at the local mall, I'm much more interested in observing the behaviors of the people who are doing life right alongside me. Early on I recognized this as an attempt to understand my students and their motivation (or lack thereof). Now, I recognize it for what it is—I'm fascinated by human behavior and psychology. What makes us act and react the way we do? What does someone's personality say about how they will handle a situation? What are the odds that I'll be wrong about the thoughts behind an action? I can think myself in circles for hours over these types of questions. I try not to, of course, but that's one of my own slippery slopes that has continued to cause problems for me since entering the promised land.

And this is a great example of how sin doesn't really leave just because we have discovered surrender. I'll probably always struggle with pride. My dad did, I do, and I see evidence of it in my nine-year-old daughter. There are likely other families who will never recognize or never have the level of pride in their lives that we do. Sin is not a one size fits all outfit. The older I get the more I realize how everyone struggles with sin, but we don't all struggle with the same sin. The point is that we will never be completely free and clear of sin or the desire to sin or the consequences of past sins. Never—on this side of heaven. What I've come to realize is that acknowledging this fact is the exact thing that will drive me into the arms of my Savior on a daily basis. The more I recognize sin and the fact that I cannot get away from it, the more I recognize how much I need a Savior. The more I recognize my need for a Savior, the more I seek a closer relationship with Christ. The more I seek that relationship the more I learn how to trust his will over my own and surrender to it. The more I surrender, the more I'm able to lead others to do the same.

My dad was incredibly cautious and taught us to be the same. It wasn't in an obsessive way—more of an observant way. He believed there was no need to get hurt if you can avoid it. This meant that we always slow down around water, we watch out for things we might run into or bump our head on, and we are constantly surveying the landscape around us for potential harm. It became almost like a game as I got older. Once I had my own child, I began teaching her to do the exact same thing. I noticed several moments when it was like we were all three having a race to determine what she could get hurt with while helping grandpa in the garage. I get that this sounds a bit wonky to some people, but when you've experienced enough life, you realize that so many hurts are things we bring on ourselves. You may not be hyper-aware of your physical surroundings, but I bet you're aware of how to stay away from the same emotional hurt you've experienced in the past. I would wager that most of us spend a great amount of time subconsciously protecting ourselves from damage we've done prior to now.

This brings us back to the small seed that we allow Satan (via the world) to plant in our soul. Unlike my method of planting—the one and done method where something gets planted and it either lives or dies—Satan is quick to fertilize any of the soil around the tiny sin seeds that he plants. I just imagine him to be the type of gardener who so desperately wants that sin seed to grow into a strong oak that he takes extra special care to water it, check the pH levels, and even spend time talking to it.

What does that look like on the outside? How can we tell when Satan is at work trying to win the state fair championship for seedlings? For me, it is usually music. Yep. I wish it weren't,

but it has been proven to me time and again that this will be my
downfall every time. It starts with spring or fall pledge drive on
my favorite national radio station. There is way more talk about
fundraising than music. (We have another Christian radio station in our area, but the reception is shady and the music is . . .
well, not always current.) I'm feeling like a little music with my
drive home. My regular station is busy talking about money, so I
decide to hit scan. It's a tiny button with a tiny purpose. Let me
rephrase that: it is a tiny seed with a huge purpose.

Inevitably the scanner will run across a country station, and I'll
stop it. You might be getting ready to tell me that Luke Combs
just wrote a song about his Bible-reading wife, or Garth and Trisha
were seen at church together, or even that Blake attributes all of
his success to his God-given talent. You're not wrong. But I'm
not them, nor will any of those things help me on my journey to
surrender. The fact is that the majority of the songs on a country
radio station will be glorifying the self over glorifying God. For
me, this is where the problems begin. When the lyrics start talking
about how I just need one more round and a night of dancing,
they might as well be handing me a ticket to a local dance hall
and a free night on my calendar. This might be because I have a
bit of a history of drinking and dancing. It might be because my
life is pretty lowkey, and that seems like just the thing to spice
it up. Or maybe it's because there is a deep longing in my heart
to let loose and not worry about what comes next. Whatever it
is, I know for certain that God is not calling me to drink and
dance my feelings away this weekend. But listening to music that
celebrates that lifestyle will start to turn my heart away from the
things I know to be true.

Country music holds ties to my past, and the nostalgia is a big
factor in why I go back to it in times of strong emotions. There
is a need to feel connected with something I once knew or the

people I once spent time with. The problem is that I was living *in* and *of* the world at that time, and even one step back could surely spell catastrophe. I know you're starting to think I'm a little bonkers for being so extreme. But y'all, I've watched it happen in my life and in the lives of others. Every moment, every day must be a choice of stepping toward God and not away. Every decision is a choice to move in a direction. We must forge a path that leads closer to our Creator and not closer to the earth he created. We must. Satan is waiting to water the seed. A seed that goes unplanted cannot grow. Don't allow the seed to be planted!

On a regular basis, I watch students rush right past the caution signs in front of them and often slip not long after. Why is this? Middle schoolers will be told to watch out for a bee hive and then proceed to purposely hit the bee hive. I could be standing over a sticky spot to block it, tell students to avoid that spot, and be physically trying to clean up the

A seed that goes unplanted cannot grow.

mess when they will inevitably walk directly into me and ask why I was on the floor. It is a confusing time both for the child going through it and the adults standing by in awe at the complete lack of good judgment. Or *any* judgment. I'd take any judgment at all at this point. It hurts my heart every time I stop to think about it because God must feel that on the deepest level possible when he watches us avoid caution sign after caution sign only to be asked to clean up our messes.

What do God's caution signs look like? Are they all in another language we can't understand? Is that why we're so quick to ignore them? It must be that they aren't loud enough or obvious enough. Or maybe they are placed over the wrong spill or in the wrong part of the building. It can't possibly be *our* fault that we don't see the warning signs God gives us. Or can it?

For a few years I've been toying with the idea that God's direction often comes from places we least expect and in ways we are not ready for, not because he doesn't love us or because he's trying to make it like a treasure hunt. I think it's because if we could just wake up with a to-do list of which choices to make that day, it would negate free will, but also negate the need to spend time with him. He is our heavenly father, but I think we all too often compare it to what we know of earthly fathers. However, the more I try to parse out that metaphor, the more it doesn't work for me. It doesn't work because God is omniscient (all-knowing), omnipotent (all-powerful), and omnipresent (all over the place). At this point, you must have realized that I often idolized my earthly father. But even I must admit that Jon Faubel in no way compares to the Creator of the universe. This means that as I grew older and realized that my dad was flawed, I could still understand that my heavenly father was and is completely flawless.

If God knows what is coming next in my life, and he knows the skills I'll need to get there, and he knows how my brain works, then wouldn't he design an alert system for me that fits all of those variables? And if he is, in fact, doing that then why is it so hard for me to hear or see the notifications he's sending? I think I mentioned that I'm not a Bible scholar, but I do understand that I am a member of the Bovidae family. (Yes, the sheep thing again.) My Shepherd cannot be far from me, or I will mess up. I will follow whatever shepherd I'm closest to. That was as true on the day of my birth as it will be on the day I pass from this world. I will not become less dependent on a shepherd. It is incumbent upon me to know *my* shepherd and be able to respond to his cues. God is not hiding from me. He wants me to follow him. He wants me to stay safe in the fold. He wants me to choose the path he has lovingly designed for me. It is my free will that I must contend with. And because that free will involves so many variables, God wants me to learn to listen for his voice and his instruction. He's not leading me on a treasure hunt; he's training me for the day he returns and calls me home. If I don't know his voice, I won't know how to get there.

Obviously, we are all now asking how to get to know a soundless voice. Am I right? I get it. I have asked myself that same question so many times. I don't think there is one single right answer to this question. I think it goes back to how we are each designed and the fact that God desires for us to be close to him.

Writing has always been a part of my life. There are countless journals which I started and then never finished. Although, can you finish something that technically has no end? Journals are designed to document stages of life or seasons we experience. Just because we do not write on every page does not mean we did not accomplish our task. But I digress. Writing my experience of passing into a life of surrender has brought a great deal of clarity for me. This is a journey that will last all of my days on earth, and writing has helped me to reflect and re-experience all that has happened. I would argue that God has used my love of writing (that he gave me) to reveal parts of his path for my life. It has also encouraged me to continue writing all of the stories I've had bottled up for years. My father's passing brought an urgency to all of the things I had been waiting to get around to. Writing is one of those things. And now God is using it to speak to me about how to explain my testimony and how to organize my thoughts and how to just finish a project. The number of skills that are growing in me because of this one faithful step of writing what I've learned is unbelievable. I challenge you to find something that you've had a passing fancy for or something you spend a lot of time doing and ask God what he wants you to see differently, where he wants you to spend your time.

Earthly wisdom comes from a multitude of experiences here on earth, right? By that logic, heavenly wisdom would be from a multitude of experiences in heaven. But we cannot get to heaven yet. So how do we make the leap from earthly experiences to heavenly experiences? Geez. If only there were written directions somewhere, a text of some sort that explained other people's experiences with God and then was good for explaining how to gain heavenly wisdom. Oh, wait! There is!

Want to know something that came along with my newfound surrender? It is something that led to surrender. Reading my Bible has been a huge blessing that God has provided in terms of direction and drawing close to him. I grew up hearing the Bible read at church and watching my parents read their Bibles at home. And I love reading. I always saw the Bible as a book of stories I already knew and then random verses I knew enough to feel comfortable that I was a "good Christian." What I've learned is that spending time in the Word allows the Holy Spirit to point things out to me and make my reading relevant to my life.

The connection between reading my Bible daily and avoiding sin seeds being planted is most likely something I don't need to even write. By now you can see the massive writing on the wall: drawing closer to God prevents sin seeds from taking hold. It reminds me of when I was young. I would have terrible nightmares and then wake up and just be sitting in the middle of my bed not wanting to go back to sleep. I would imagine a den of snakes was under my bed, demons were in the corners of the room, and the path to my mom's bed across the hall was too treacherous to even attempt. In those moments I would say out loud the name of Jesus over and over. I didn't understand a lot about spirituality, but I knew darkness could not reside where there was light. Satan's demons could not exist where the name of Jesus was spoken. So I would say those things into the darkness. Even into my twenties, alone in my studio apartment in a foreign country, awakened by a horrible dream and not wanting to go back to sleep, I spoke the name of Jesus into the darkness. At thirty-eight years old, I remember the first time I awoke in the middle of the night to hear my daughter saying the name of Jesus into the darkness, letting the demons know that she had been claimed by the Most High God, and they were not welcome in our home.

Y'all. That's the power of the Holy Spirit that lives inside us. That deep, guttural, unexplainable level of understanding that just speaking the name of Jesus will bring peace. Being able to fall back to sleep after a nightmarish episode and still waking up the next morning feeling refreshed. That's the power of the Holy Spirit living inside of us.

And I waited forty years to stop the wandering. It's baffling.

Author Suggestion: Are you wandering (with an 'a') or wondering (with an 'o')? Either way, it might be productive for you to make a list of your sin seeds. What are Satan's greatest hits in your life? Pray over your list - daily.

Chapter 7

Who is your Moses?

There's no question in my mind that my dad is the Moses of my life. This was not always obvious to me because I don't think I truly understood Moses until I read the entire section of the Bible where he leads the Israelites through the wilderness. Having grown up in Sunday school—one which must have had a substantial felt board budget—I had seen the story of Moses in the basket, Moses speaking to Pharaoh, Moses parting the Red Sea, and Moses striking the rock numerous times. As I got older I even heard sermons that tried to reveal a deep, dark secret by recounting how Moses had a stammering problem and how God can use our human weaknesses to do his work. But I never in my whole life had connected Moses to my dad.

The following comes from the end of Deuteronomy. Just to recap: Exodus is where Moses leads the people out of slavery; Leviticus is where the laws for God's people are laid out; Numbers is a retelling of laws but also an explanation of the tribes and their responsibilities; Deuteronomy is repeating all of the laws as the Israelites are drawing near to the end of the forty years of wandering; and Joshua is directly after Moses dies and Joshua leads the people into the promised land.

> Then Moses climbed Mount Nebo from the plains of Moab to the top of Pisgah, across from Jericho. There the LORD showed him the whole land—from Gilead to Dan, all of Naphtali, the territory of Ephraim and Manasseh, all the land of Judah as far as the Mediterranean Sea, the Negev and the whole region from the Valley of Jericho, the City of Palms, as far as Zoar. Then the LORD said to him, "This is the land I promised on oath to Abraham, Isaac and Jacob when I said, 'I will give it to your descendants.' I have let you see it with your eyes, but you will not cross over into it."
>
> And Moses the servant of the LORD died there in Moab, as the LORD had said. He buried him in Moab, in the valley opposite Beth Peor, but to this day no one knows where his grave is. Moses was a hundred and twenty years old when he died, yet his eyes were not weak nor his strength gone. The Israelites grieved for Moses in the plains of Moab thirty days, until the time of weeping and mourning was over.
>
> Now Joshua son of Nun was filled with the spirit of wisdom because Moses had laid his hands on him. So the Israelites listened to him and did what the LORD had commanded Moses.
>
> Since then, no prophet has risen in Israel like Moses, whom the LORD knew face to face, who did all those signs and wonders the LORD sent him to do in Egypt—to Pharaoh and to all his officials and to his whole land. For no one has ever shown the mighty power or performed the awesome deeds that Moses did in the sight of all Israel. (Deut. 34:1–11)

When I read that for the first time—only a year ago—I about lost my mind. I almost spit out my coffee. This man, Moses, was chosen by God to lead an entire population of Israelites. And not just a few towns over. No. He was tasked with moving them far away, on foot, through barren land. He was God's messenger and probably the original reason we have the saying, "Don't shoot the messenger," given the things he had to report to these people.

And because of one misstep, he can only *see* the promised land. He will not be allowed to cross into the land flowing with milk and honey with his people. Do you know what that misstep was, incidentally? He needed to get water from a rock for the people he was leading. God told him to speak to the rock and water would flow. Instead, Moses struck the rock with his staff. Water still flowed, but Moses' future in the promised land changed. If this great man was banished from the promised land for the difference between speaking and striking - what kind of hope is there for me? I've made far more than one misstep. Of course, I've never been allowed to speak with God face to face either—so there's that.

But there is powerful imagery here. A man toils to bring a people to the promised land and then dies on a mountain, in an unknown place, unable to enjoy the bounty. It sounded so unfair. I was outraged. Was it all for naught? Really?

As I ruminated on this revelation, I realized that Moses' life was about bringing glory to God, not to him-

None of it is supposed to be about us.

self. It was authentic leadership in every sense of the word. It is the embodiment of what we are called to do with our own lives; surrender to God's will, lead others to safety, and die in an unknown grave. None of it is supposed to be about us. It is about Christ in us and the people around us. If we get it right, if we truly get it right, we will die at peace knowing we labored until the very end, ensuring those entrusted to our care were delivered safe and sound.

I have a lot of feelings about my dad not being here on earth to experience all of these recent spiritual breakthroughs with me. After all, he was the example I followed my whole life and the man who would set the standard for our family and the person who walked through so much of my rebellion with me. Why did he not see me thriving in this land that he worked so hard to lead me to?

I'm not certain, but I think it might be because I looked to his leadership so much that it needed to be taken away before I would be able to allow the Holy Spirit to lead me instead. God, in his infinite wisdom and planning, knew that I had to be completely broken and acknowledge my need for him before I would cross the threshold into surrender. And my eyes had been fixed on my dad's example instead of the Holy Spirit.

Moses was the earthly example God gave the Israelites to help communicate his plans for them, lead them through the wilderness, and reprimand them when they turned away. It was Moses who solidified their escape from slavery. God allowed Moses to perform miracles (or God performed the miracles through Moses? I've never quite sorted that out), like the parting of the Red Sea. Moses was human; he made plenty of mistakes, but he was chosen and never seemed to stop trying to follow what God had for him. All of these characteristics sound incredibly familiar, as I was given an earthly father who followed the exact same pattern.

Do you have a Moses? Is there someone who you view as a spiritual leader in your life? Someone you would follow through the wilderness for half of your life even though you know they are an imperfect human?

Can we take it further and ask, "Am I the Moses for someone else?" If your answer is automatically "No," then I would challenge you to ask yourself why you believe that to be true. Maybe you don't realize there is someone following your lead. Maybe you don't feel as if your leadership is worth following. Maybe you're so busy trying to get it together that you don't even have time to look around to see who is watching. I would ask you to proceed with caution. Someone is always watching your example—whether it is leading them toward Christ or not.

During a particularly difficult season I was surrounded by friends who wanted to help but didn't know how. They grew tired of my inability to talk about anything except how poorly my marriage was going. Through no fault of their own, many of them did not have the time or energy to commit to my issues. I understood completely. I didn't even want to be who I was during that time. Looking back, what I'm most disappointed in is the fact that I could have been leading others to Christ the entire time, but instead, I was consumed by my inadequacies and reaching for anything that could soothe my aching heart. Anything except Jesus, of course.

> **Someone is always watching your example—whether it is leading them toward Christ or not.**

Let me clarify. I am not disappointed that I wasn't going on mission trips or that I wasn't teaching Sunday school. I am not upset that I wasn't praying over everyone and being a spiritual leader. There are times when we need to lean on others and give ourselves time to heal. What bothered me is that my friends had to watch me constantly reach out and try to fix my problems in ways that were not God-honoring. It's like the faith I thought I had, had disappeared and was replaced with faith in my friends' advice, faith in worldly endeavors, and faith in just about anything other than the saving power of Jesus. Walking where I'm walking now, I see how that time would have been so much less tumultuous had I truly understood surrender and had my faith been rooted deeper than going to church on Sundays, vacation Bible school songs, and quick prayers before mealtime. Friend, believing in God's saving grace is not the same as living in it daily.

In that whole season of separation and divorce, I was solidifying—not only in my heart but in the hearts of those around me who were watching—the world's opinion of how to get over something. I was like any other believer who held fast to a checklist of what makes me a Christian while simultaneously living a life that was wholly un-surrendered to a Savior. And I have no idea how many people's hearts were left in the wake of my tidal wave of bad decisions and unbelieving ways. Collateral damage is always at play. Someone is always watching and taking their cues from us—even people we don't know.

So I ask again, who is your Moses? Who are you allowing to lead you through your wilderness? Is it someone who has truly surrendered to Christ, or is it someone who is close to you here on earth but who—through no fault of their own and without even knowing it—is leading you in Christ-less circles?

Likewise, who are you leading through the wilderness? Are you allowing God to lead them through your surrender to his will? Or are you allowing the world to guide them through your shallow faith?

> *Author Suggestion: Meditate on this idea of leading and being led. Consider the questions that have been asked about your life and surrender. Is there a trusted friend who could help guide you in discovering your truth?*

Chapter 8

I Want to Be Like Anna

There is this incredible story in Luke (New Testament) that tells the reader of a woman named Anna. Are you familiar with Anna? She was a widow who fasted and prayed. She devoted her life to following God. I want to be like her.

There are not a lot of details about Anna. Here is what we know from Luke chapter 2.

> There was also a prophet, Anna, the daughter of Penuel, of the tribe of Asher. She was very old; she had lived with her husband seven years after her marriage, and then was a widow until she was eighty-four. She never left the temple but worshiped night and day, fasting and praying. Coming up to them at that very moment, she gave thanks to God and spoke about the child to all who were looking forward to the redemption of Jerusalem. (vv. 36–38)

I'm not a widow; however, I am single. And I was married for five years. For the first time in my life, I find myself having the desire to expectantly wait for God from now until the day I die. There is something so beautiful about Anna, who goes about her daily life in a way that seeks to find God in everything. She was one of the first—outside of Mary, Joseph, and the gang that gathered at Jesus' birth—to recognize Jesus as the Messiah. Can you imagine being so attuned to God's presence that out of thousands of people, you are the one who recognizes his Son in a temple?

I'm trying to imagine what that would look like in modern times. Is it possible to recognize God working among all of the noise and crowds? Would anyone believe me, even if they knew I had a history of following the Holy Spirit? I wonder about this because sometimes I don't even believe, myself. I pray for the Holy Spirit to guide me and then when I think I feel moved in a direction, I often second guess it. I'm learning to go with it. I'm learning to differentiate between thoughts in my own mind, sin seeds from Satan, and the guidance of the Holy Spirit. There's no way to get it right every time (at least not on our own) is there? It's a tricky business. Especially when it involves someone else.

> **Is it possible to recognize God working among all of the noise and crowds?**

Recently, a small-group member asked for prayer about a decision to join church leadership. As I listened to his explanation of the process so far and what it means moving forward, I was on board. There was a small tug at my heart when he mentioned the time commitment—this is something I often shy away from because I've had past experience with taking on too much. What I've learned is that we make time for what is important to us, and we cannot be the guardians of someone else's schedule. He was clearly aware of what would be required and was prayerfully considering everything. Nothing moved me to say anything, and no thoughts came to mind.

And so it was . . . for several days. I didn't even think about it again. Life moved on. Saturday morning, three days after this potential move was mentioned, I was praying after my First 5 study. (Have I mentioned how amazing First 5 is?) During my prayer, thoughts of this person's move to leadership began to enter my mind. It was just questions. I honestly couldn't understand why those questions had anything to do with me or why I would need those answers. So I just sat with it for a minute. I finished praying only to begin again—asking for guidance from the Holy Spirit. What was I supposed to do with these questions? Surely I wasn't being asked to grill this family about their intentions. Why me? There are other, much more qualified people to have this conversation with them. In fact, they've probably already answered these questions. This is not really any of my business. Many more people know them so much better.

Here's what I know. At this point in my life, I'm afraid of being disobedient to the calling of the Holy Spirit. What I was being asked to share was not my opinion or advice. It was simply a list of questions that the receiver can take and use however they wish. By the time I finished praying about what I was supposed to do with these questions I knew a quick email would be the best route. It would allow me to state everything clearly, and the Holy Spirit could guide the process from there. To be honest, this may have been the easy way out. I have to believe, though, that God knows my heart and my intentions and chose me for a reason. Of course, then I had to fight back the pride that wanted to creep up and remind me of what a great job I'm doing of listening to the Holy Spirit. It was an intense morning.

I sent the email. I got a response some time later. I will probably never really know the outcome of those questions. Quite honestly, it matters not to me one way or the other. I want to support and pray over and love on my community in every way possible. I've learned enough to know that so many of the things we get bent out of shape over have no real significance in our lives. None of it matters. If this small-group member becomes a different level of leader in the church, cool, cool. If he decides not to, cool, cool. This one event is not going to change the fact that God is still in control. God can remove him or place him in leadership anytime he sees fit. At the end of the day, it's about being obedient—day by day, step by step. If I'm not obedient to what I'm called to do, then God will bless someone else who is watching intently for their next mission.

If I'm to be like Anna, I need to be in constant prayer and fasting. My life should be a model of servanthood. Boldness would be nothing but an everyday occurrence for me because my heart and actions would be led by the Holy Spirit and not the things of this world. If I'm to be like Anna, I have a laundry list of items that need to change. And it becomes overwhelming to be like someone else, like one of the few women who are mentioned in the Bible. So I take a breath and remind myself that while emulation is a great way to learn, it is not my single purpose for living. My story will not mirror Anna's, and that's okay. For starters, my marriage died—not my spouse. These are two very different ways for a union to end.

> **If I'm to be like Anna, I need to be in constant prayer and fasting.**

If you've never been through a divorce, you can't imagine the pain that accompanies it. Much like the loss of a loved one, divorce is a life event that forms an unwanted club of survivors. It forces us into a category. And that brings its own set of emotions. To know that something may have been within your control but you failed is a whole new level of shame and guilt. As a Christian, the shame was extra pronounced, and the place where I wanted to go for refuge had become the place I was too embarrassed to attend—church. Church was full of people who were getting it right, and I was left—left alone, left without my child half the time, and left feeling like I should have done more.

There's no better way to describe it than brokenness. It's a point where a broken world has found its way into broken people who then create a broken home. There are many tragedies in this world that could be prevented and there are many lies that the enemy has woven into the fabric of our culture. The idea that divorce is best for all involved is one of the most treacherous.

It was a rough season. The shame, guilt, embarrassment, and grief were enough to take down even the strongest believer. I found myself feeling hopeless on a daily basis. You know how people say they can barely keep their head above water? Going through a divorce was like being pushed under by enormous waves and only having seconds to suck in a breath before going under again. The difference in my story—maybe—is that the enormous waves began crushing me some time around the middle of my first year of marriage. Can anyone else relate to the soul-crushing shame of divorce? It might not be divorce. It might be the loss of a child, a past that won't leave you alone, financial devastation, or a plethora of other worldly hurts. We have all been through something that has left us hopeless. And if you haven't yet, don't worry, your time will come.

My head knew how to access God, but my heart did not. I did what most Christians probably do—I started making mental checklists and seeking advice from more experienced believers. I was positive that if I prayed more, read my Bible more, and invested my time at church more I would come out victorious in the end. The entire time that I was trying so desperately to grow closer to God, I was actually creating more space between us by walking away. Walking away looked like making decisions based on my own logic, not on listening for direction. It looked like going through the motions with no heart behind them. Yes, I now know what Paul says about doing things without love and how it will yield no result. Yes, I now know that there is a difference between accepting Christ and actually allowing the Holy Spirit to guide you. Yes, I'm now well-aware that I was missing the whole point—the boat, the meaning. And still . . . I just simply did not know how to get there—wherever *there* was.

Now I'm on the other side and yet, I feel like it's the tip of the iceberg. You know when people say, "We can never understand the depth of God's love"? And we all nod along and say amen when inside we are actually wondering if we even feel God's love on a minuscule level because it feels as if it's just something that is supposed to happen but isn't actually tangible here on earth? Am I the only one?

I grew up in the most loving, disciplined, discipled home a person could find or create and I still didn't grasp God's love. I just thought that was why we had faith. I honestly believed that it was simply a gap between faith and reality. That this gap was a natural part of our relationship with God. That, in theory, we could begin to close the distance, but in reality, most people were perfectly content knowing about God's love and reading about God's love without ever experiencing God's love. Or it would just be something I felt in times of difficulty or when I was amazed by childbirth or in those rare mountaintop experiences. But every day? Like, laying my head down at night and feeling loved by the Creator of the universe? Walking through my day and my thoughts turning to my heavenly Father faster than they do to juicy gossip? I could never have fathomed that it would be something I longed for. And because I didn't realize this could exist—I had trouble taking steps to grasp it. In fact,

I didn't take the steps at all. That's the big secret: There. Are. No. Steps.

I know, I know. List-lovers everywhere just gasped in shock at the idea that their carefully created to-dos will actually not work in this particular pursuit. I shouldn't say they won't work. I don't know for sure. But I would guess, based on my experience and what I've heard others share, that a list might be counterproductive in this case.

I wonder if Anna ever struggled with her own belief. I mean, at the time when she lived, women were viewed as less than, and widows had little protection. I wonder if that's how she ended up at the temple every day. I'm curious to know if her earthly circumstances were what God used to draw her closer to him. If that's the case, then Anna and I are more alike than I once believed. To take it a step further, it seems like every story I read in the Old Testament is about earthly circumstances that create a situation in which humans are being drawn closer to their Creator. So what if the entire Bible was written for the sole purpose of showing us that we are not the only ones? What if God filled people with an urgency to write about how much we need a Savior? And then BAM! In the second chapter of Matthew that Savior shows up and the world is forever changed. But you know what I notice that doesn't change? The stories in the New Testament do the same thing as the stories in the Old Testament. They put on display God's power in drawing his people closer to himself.

What if I just go with it? What if God is not asking me to be like Anna in any other way except to acknowledge how much I need his protection and to draw near to him? Again, I'm being moved in the direction of surrender. I am being shown that strength comes from being dependent on God and not finding ways to depend on myself. I'm recognizing that my flaws can be the very things that will pull me to his side and under his wing. I have been found - not with my own strength, or my own logic, or my own anything. My once reckless behavior that could have led me into the depths of hell if not for a Savior that chose to save me. I now want to love that Savior with reckless abandon. And he chooses to love me even more than that. Cory Asbury recorded a song with these lyrics:

> *Oh, the overwhelming, never-ending, reckless love of God.*
> *It chases me down, fights 'til I'm found, leaves the ninety-nine.*
> *I couldn't earn it. I don't deserve it. Still you give yourself away.*
> *Oh, the overwhelming, never-ending, reckless love of God.*

That song gives me chills and brings out the super-loud car singing that one only does with the windows rolled tightly up. Not long ago, somewhere deep inside of me was stirred up and I performed loud car singing at church—around other people! Later that day I wondered what would happen if we all felt comfortable enough to fill our lungs and as loudly as possible sing about the love of God and all he has done in our lives. That would require

It would require overwhelming, never-ending, reckless worship.

an understanding of what he has done and who he truly is. It would require overwhelming, never-ending, reckless worship. Not just with my singing but with my daily choices, with my relationships, with my money, and with my time.

If I am to live like Anna or at least emulate the parts of her life that will draw me closer to our Savior, I need to live a life of prayer and fasting. I need to be near the temple and the teachings of Jesus. I must be living a life waiting for the arrival of the Messiah. When I cross-reference my personal experience with what I've read about Anna, it is my belief that I will continue to find that my life becomes less about my earthly desires and more about drawing others to the Holy Spirit inside of me. It will be less about who I'm in relationship with and more about how the Holy Spirit wants to speak through me to those people. The power to heal, to cast out demons, and to love my neighbors resides inside of me. Am I living a life worthy of that power? Am I living a life of surrender? At the end of the day, nothing else matters.

> **Author Suggestion: Are you living in surrender? Are you truly seeking God's will or simply asking for a blessing over decisions you've made based on your own logic and skill? Are you even open to the possibility that God's love is deeper than you can even imagine?*

Acknowledgments

These pages came together in my mind and then on paper. Eventually, these words found their way into chapters and an entire book. I'd like to thank the following people who contributed to the process:

Those who have read, re-read, and offered feedback at various points. (I would list names, but the amount of support has been so great that I fear I will miss someone.)

The members of my small group—without your patience and grace I am convinced the journey on these pages would have taken twice as long. I'm grateful that you are my people.

My editor, Amy Barham. You took a muddled mess of experience and straightened it out to be the best representation of my story.

My formatter, Michael Williams, who waited patiently for a new author who had no idea what each piece of the process would entail. And then created a piece of visual art from the manuscript I handed him.

My graphic designer, Natalie Holland, who graciously worked me into her hectic schedule. I am thankful for your effort and all of the dinner meetings.

My cover illustrator, Juliann Chatman, who is an amazing daughter and fantastic artist. I cannot wait to see where God leads you and the masterpieces you will create.

www.ingramcontent.com/pod-product-compliance
Lightning Source LLC
LaVergne TN
LVHW051150080426

835508LV00021B/2566